D1022750

Hebrews
AND James

FAITH
WORKS

Translated from Greek and Aramaic Texts

DR. BRIAN SIMMONS

BroadStreet
PUBLISHING

Hebrews and James: Faith Works, The Passion Translation®
Translated from the Greek and Aramaic texts by Dr. Brian Simmons

Published by BroadStreet Publishing Group, LLC
Racine, Wisconsin, USA
BroadStreetPublishing.com

© 2014, 2016 The Passion Translation®

ISBN-13: 978-1-4245-4960-3 (paperback)
ISBN-13: 978-1-4245-4963-4 (e-book)

Cover and interior design by Garborg Design Works, Inc. | www.garborgdesign.com
Interior typesetting by Katherine Lloyd | www.theDESKonline.com

Printed in the United States of America
16 17 18 19 20   10 9 8 7 6 5

Translator's Introduction to Hebrews

AT A GLANCE

Author: Unknown, but possibly Paul, Barnabas, Apollos, or Priscilla

Audience: Christians converted from Judaism

Date: AD 50–64

Type of Literature: A sermon in the form of a letter

Major Themes: Jesus, the Old Testament, faith, perseverance, and heaven

Outline:

Prologue — 1:1–4
Jesus' Superiority over Angels and Moses — 1:5–4:13
Jesus' Superior Priesthood — 4:14–7:28
Jesus' Superior Sacrifice and Covenant — 8:1–10:18
A Call to Persevere — 10:19–12:29
Final Instructions and Greetings — 13:1–25

ABOUT HEBREWS

The book of Hebrews presents the magnificent Jesus on every page!

The light of the Messiah brings truth out from the shadows and shines it brightly for all to see. It is written for every believer today, for we have crossed over from darkness to light and from doubt to faith. The name Hebrews means, "those who crossed over." We have passed from shadows to substance and from doubt to the reality of faith. What once was a symbol has now become substance, for all the pictures of the Old Testament have found their fulfillment in Jesus.

Hebrews takes us into the Holy of Holies as we come to him as priests, lovers, and worshipers. You will never be the same again when you absorb the light of God that shines from every chapter.

Jesus is the theme of Hebrews. You must learn from him and draw closer to him in order to understand the depth of this book, for Jesus is the language of God! When God now speaks to us, he speaks in the vocabulary of Jesus Christ. All of the Bible points to him. Can we truly understand the Bible if we don't come to him?

Hebrews is a divinely inspired composition given to show us the magnificence of Jesus as our glorious High Priest. He is greater than the Law, the angels, the system of temple worship, and greater than any high priest or religious structure. Because our Royal Priest gave his sacred blood for us, we now have unrestricted access to the Holiest Place of All. With no veil and nothing hindering our intimacy with God, we can come with an unbelievable boldness to his mercy-throne where we encounter enough grace to empower us through every difficulty. We find our true life in his presence.

Heaven's words are now before you, so read them with spiritual hunger and a passion to embrace truth, and live it out by the grace of Jesus, our Messiah.

God will help you!

PURPOSE

The purpose of the pastor's sermon is evident the further you read his letter: he is trying to prevent those he's addressing from abandoning their Christian faith and return to Judaism. Along the way, the author teaches them—and us—about the superiority of Christ above the religious institutions of Moses and the Old Testament. The sermon-letter is filled with references to the old sacrificial system and priesthood of ancient Israel and explains how Jesus' death has replaced this old religious system—making it the perfect book to understand how Jesus' story fulfills Israel's story!

AUTHOR AND AUDIENCE

The book of Hebrews was most likely written sometime around AD 50–64. It had to have been written prior to Clement of Rome citing it as inspired (AD 95) and before the Roman war that destroyed the temple in AD 67–70. Though Hebrew's true authorship is unknown, the earliest church fathers taught that Hebrews was written in Hebrew by Paul for the Jewish people. Eusebius (AD 260–339) refers to an even earlier apostolic father, Clement of Alexandria (AD 150–211), who confirms without question that Paul wrote Hebrews in the Hebrew language for the Hebrew people. (See Eusebius *History, Book VI: XIV.*) More recent scholarship, however, has begun to question this and speculate that it was written by Barnabas, Apollos, Priscilla, or another one of Paul's close associates.

Regardless of who wrote it, we are more certain about who read it—or rather, who first heard it read out loud, because Hebrews seems to be more of a sermon contained in a letter. The inscription placed on the original document is "To the Hebrews," and the major themes point to a group of Jewish Christians who may have been getting cold feet, wondering if they should return back to non-Christian Judaism. This sermon-letter is so steeped in ancient Jewish practices that it seems very likely the author is addressing Christians converted from Judaism. And yet, the letter still speaks to us, because Christ's sacrifice and new covenant is better than religious rules and rituals!

MAJOR THEMES

Christology: Christology is the study of the Christ, the Messiah, and this letter is a full-on course in our heavenly Savior! The revelation of Jesus fills the pages of Hebrews and it will set you free! He is our magnificent High Priest who is greater than Moses, greater than any sacrifice ever offered, greater than any prophet of old. He perfects our faith until we rise with him into the heavenly realm of priestly ministry. He warns us of turning back into ritual and religion, forgetting all the treasures of our faith. He stirs us to enter into the full rest by seeing Jesus alone as our perfection before the Father.

The Old Covenant Fulfilled: One of the central themes of Hebrews is the relationship of the new covenant established by the blood of Jesus, the Messiah to the old or "first covenant." Look at all the Old Testament imagery the pastor uses: Moses, the high priest, Melchizedek, the priestly order of Aaron, offerings and sacrifices, the ark of the covenant, and the Most Holy Place. Even though we are far removed from the original religious system of rules and rituals found in the Old Testament, we cannot afford to ignore the pastor's message: The High Priesthood of Jesus is inherent to his identity as our all-sufficient Rescuer and Revealer!

The Reality of Heaven: The Hebrews sermon often speaks about heaven's reality. The pastor reveals it's the place where God keeps his throne; to be in heaven means to be in God's very presence; in it are the names of everyone whom God calls his own; and it is the place where our ultimate redemption and atonement took place. This last revelation of heaven is especially important, because Hebrews explains the old religious order of rules and rituals is no longer necessary because of the final sacrifice made for all people. All God commanded under the first covenant on earth became obsolete and disappeared thanks to what Jesus accomplished in heaven! The heavenly temple is where our ultimate salvation was accomplished, of which the earthly one could not.

Definition and Practice of Faith: Nowhere is there a better definition and explanation of faith in the New Testament than in the sermon-letter of Hebrews: "Now faith brings our hopes into reality and becomes the foundation needed to acquire the things we long for. It is all the evidence required to prove what is still unseen" (11:1). This is a far cry from the traditional understanding that faith is merely belief. Biblical faith claims a confidence beyond our own because it rests in the character of God, the foundation of our faith. Part of practicing faith is persevering in it. Despite the fact we live in a world that refuses to acknowledge God and opposes the church, we are called to persevere in our faith in him, just like the "great witnesses who encircle us like clouds"! Hebrews warns against turning away in rebellion and unbelief, telling us the very divine message which saved us is the same one that will condemn us if we do.

A WORD ABOUT THE PASSION TRANSLATION

The message of God's story is timeless; the Word of God doesn't change. But the methods by which that story is communicated should be timely; the vessels that steward God's Word can and should change.

One of those timely methods and vessels is Bible translations. Bible translations are both a gift and a problem. They give us the words God spoke through his servants, but words can become very poor containers for revelation—they leak! Over time the words change from one generation to the next.

There is no such thing as a truly literal translation of the Bible, for there is not an equivalent language that perfectly conveys the meaning of the biblical text except as it is understood in its original cultural and linguistic setting. Therefore, a translation can be a problem. The problem, however, is solved when we seek to transfer meaning, and not merely words, from the original text to the receptor language.

The Passion Translation is a groundbreaking attempt to re-introduce the passion and fire of the Bible to the English reader. It doesn't merely convey the original, literal meaning of words. It expresses God's passion for people and his world by translating the original, life-changing message of God's Word for modern readers.

God longs to have his Word expressed in every language in a way that would unlock the passion of his heart. Our goal is to trigger inside every English speaker an overwhelming response to the truth of the Bible. This is a heart-level translation, from the passion of God's heart to the passion of your heart.

We pray and trust this version of God's Word will kindle in you a burning, passionate desire for him and his heart, while impacting the Church for years to come!

—Dr. Brian Simmons

Hebrews

$\mathcal{One}$

Jesus, the Language of God

¹Throughout our history God has spoken to our ancestors by his prophets in many different ways. The revelation he gave them was only a fragment at a time, building one truth upon another.ᵃ ²But to us living in these last days,ᵇ God now speaks to us openly in the language of a Son,ᶜ the appointed Heir of everything, for through him God created the panorama of all things and all time.ᵈ

³The Son is the dazzling radiance of God's splendor,ᵉ the exact expression of God's true nature—his mirror image!ᶠ He holds the universeᵍ together and expands itʰ by the mighty power of his spoken word.ⁱ He

---

a 1:1 Implied in the text. The Greek is "God spoke in different times in different parts." That is, he reveals one piece and then another, like pieces of a puzzle, with one piece complementing the other. The Aramaic can be translated "God spoke to our ancestors by all methods and at any price" or "in every way, shape, and form." That is, by sample and by example God reveals his ways progressively, building on previous understandings, leading us into Christ's fullness.

b 1:2 This phrase, often used by the prophets of the Old Testament, speaks of our current time in human history between Acts 2 (Pentecost) and the coming again of Christ.

c 1:2 Or "he has spoken through a Son." We speak in English; God speaks in "Son," for Jesus is the language of God. The Sonship of Jesus is the language he now uses to speak to us.

d 1:2 Or "the complete period of all existence." The Aramaic is, "universes." Both the concept of "all things," and, "all times (the ages)," are implied in the text.

e 1:3 Or "the out-shining (effulgence) of God's glory. The Aramaic is "He is the Sprout of God, the image of his glory."

f 1:3 Or "the Son is God's mirror image and exact expression (the reflection of God)."

g 1:3 The Aramaic is "He is Almighty."

h 1:3 The Greek word *phero*, has as its primary meaning "to carry along" or "to move (something) forward." Forward motion is implied. See *Strong's Concordance* 5342.

i 1:3 This is the Greek word, *rhema*, which is the sayings of the Son, or *his spoken word*.

accomplished for us the complete cleansing of sins,[a] and then took his seat on the highest throne at the right hand[b] of the majestic One.[c]

Jesus, Greater than Angels

[4]He is infinitely greater than angels, for he inherited a rank and a Name[d] far greater than theirs. [5]For God has never said to any angel what he said to Jesus:

> **"You are my favored Son, today I have fathered you."**[e]

And this:

> **"I will be the Father to him, and he will be the Son to me."**[f]

[6]And again, when he brought his firstborn Son into the world:

> **"Let all my angels bow down before him**
> **and kiss him in worship."**[g]

[7]And about his angels he says,

> **"I make my angels swift winds,**
> **and my ministers[h] fiery flames."**[i]

[8]But about his Son, he called him "God,"[j] saying,

---

a 1:3 Or "Because he had accomplished our purification from sins (atonement)."

b 1:3 That is, the place of highest honor and authority. See Psalm 110:1. Some have proposed that v.3 is an ancient Christian hymn that summarizes our faith.

c 1:3 Or "the Majesty," a periphrasis for God.

d 1:4 This is *Ha Shem*, in the Aramaic, the common title for God. This elevates the meaning of the passage much clearer than Greek, for Jesus is now given the "Name," that is, he has the title of God (*Ha Shem*, the Name).

e 1:5 The Aramaic can be translated, "Every day I beget you." See Psalm 2:7, 12.

f 1:5 See 2 Samuel 7:14; 1 Chronicles 17:13.

g 1:6 See Psalm 97:7. The Greek word used for worship *proskuneo*, includes three concepts: "To bow," "to kiss," and "to pay homage (worship)." All three are included here. This seems to be referring to Christ's birth, however, some interpret this to be when Jesus was exalted and ascended into heaven.

h 1:7 The Greek word *leitourgos*, means "those who read the liturgy" or "priests."

i 1:7 See Psalm 104:4.

j 1:8 Clearly implied in the text and made explicit.

"Your throne, O God, endures forever and ever
and you will rule your kingdom
with justice and righteousness,[a]
⁹For you have cherished righteousness
and detested lawlessness.
For this reason, God, your God, has anointed you[b]
and poured out the oil of bliss on you[c]
more than on any of your friends."

¹⁰And he called him Lord,[d] saying,

"Lord, you formed the earth in the beginning[e]
and with your own hands you crafted the cosmos.[f]
¹¹They will both one day disappear,
but you will remain forever!
They will all fade like a worn-out garment,
¹²And they will be changed like clothes,
and you will fold them up and put them away.
But you are 'I Am.'[g]
You never change, years without end!"[h]

¹³And God has never said this to any of his angels:

---

a 1:8 The Greek used here can mean either justice or righteousness; this translation includes both. The text is literally "the righteous scepter is the scepter of your kingdom."

b 1:9 The word, Messiah, means "Anointed One." There is a clear and unmistakable poetic play on words by reading the Aramaic (*Mashkhakh Alaha Alahakh Meshka*, almost a complete reversing of the sounds of the first into the second), that is lost in the Greek.

c 1:9 Or "the oil of rejoicing." See Psalm 45:6–7.

d 1:10 Clearly implied in the text and made explicit.

e 1:10 See Psalm 102:25–27.

f 1:10 See Psalm 8:1–3.

g 1:12 As translated from the Aramaic, which is literally "you are as you are." This is a variation of the name of God revealed to Moses in Exodus 3:14, "I Am who I Am." There is an obvious connection here to that incident and endorses the truth that the pre-incarnate Christ was the One who appeared in the burning bush.

h 1:12 The Aramaic is "the years will not age you."

> "Take your seat next to me at my right hand
> until I force your whispering enemies[a]
> to be a rug under your feet."[b]

[14]What role then, do the angels have? The angels are spirit-messengers sent by God to serve those who are going to be saved.[c]

---

a 1:13 As translated from the Aramaic.
b 1:13 Or "a footstool for your feet." See Psalm 110:1. Placing the feet on a defeated enemy was a gesture of triumph. See Joshua 10:24; 1 Kings 5:3.
c 1:14 The Aramaic is "The angels are spirit-winds-of-ministry sent to minister to those destined to receive salvation." The angels are glad to minister to us, for they see us "in Christ."

Two

A Warning Not to Drift from Truth

¹This is why it is so crucial that we be all the more engaged and attentive to the truths[a] that we have heard so that we do not drift off course. ²For if the message of the law[b] spoken and confirmed by angels[c] brought a just penalty to every disobedient violation; ³then how would we expect to escape punishment[d] if we despise the very truths that give us life?[e] The Lord himself was the first to announce these things, and those who heard him firsthand confirmed their accuracy. ⁴Then God added his witness to theirs. He validated their ministry with signs, astonishing wonders, all kinds of powerful miracles,[f] and by the gifts of the Holy Spirit,[g] which he distributed as he desired.

---

a 2:1 Or "things," by implication *truths.*

b 2:2 Implied in the text and made explicit.

c 2:2 See Deuteronomy 33:2; Psalm 68:17; Acts 7:38, 53. Angels participated in the giving of the Torah.

d 2:3 Implied in the text and made explicit.

e 2:2 As translated from the Aramaic. This appears to be a quote from Deuteronomy 32:47. The Greek is "how will we escape if we neglect such a great salvation." There are six significant warnings in Hebrews. 1) Here in 2:1–4 we are warned not to drift away from the power of our great salvation. 2) In 3:7–4:13 we are warned about failing to enter into the faith-rest life with the failure of the Israelites in the wilderness as an example. 3) In 5:11–6:12 we are warned to be devoted to the full assurance of our hope until life's end. 4) In 10:23–39 we are warned of not sinning willfully after we have received the truth. 5) In 12:1–17 we are given the warning of God's correction as our faithful Father. 6) In 12:25–29 we are warned not to close our hearts to the voice of the One who speaks from heaven.

f 2:4 Signs, wonders, and miracles, were all components of the ministries of the New Testament believer. There is no place in Scripture to indicate that any of the works of Jesus or his apostles should not be seen today. See John 14:12; Acts 2:22, 43; 5:12; 6:8; 8:13; Romans 15:19; 2 Corinthians 12:12; Galatians 3:5.

g 2:4 Or "by distributions of the Holy Spirit." The Greek word for distribution is often used for dividing an inheritance. The word *gifts* is implied in the text and made explicit.

Jesus, and the Destiny of Believers

⁵For God will not place the coming world, of which we speak, under the government of angels. ⁶But the Scriptures affirm:

> **What is man that you would even think about him,**
> **or care about Adam's race.**
> ⁷**You made him lower than the angels for a little while.**[a]
> **You placed your glory and honor**
> **upon his head as a crown.**
> **And you have given him dominion**
> **over the works of your hands,**[b]
> ⁸**For you have placed everything under his authority.**[c]

This means that God has left nothing outside the control of his Son, even if presently we have yet to see this accomplished. ⁹But we see Jesus, who as a man,[d] lived for a short time lower than the angels and has now been crowned with glorious honor because of what he suffered in his death. For it was by God's grace[e] that he experienced death's bitterness on behalf of everyone![f]

---

a 2:7 See Psalm 8:4–6. The Aramaic can be translated "Who is man that you would give a thought toward him, for whom the Son of Man should be pledged (to be offered for them)." The phrase "son of man" is used in the New Testament consistently for Jesus Christ, the "Son of Man." The Hebrew text of Psalm 8 refers to man being made a little lower than *Elohim* (God), which can also mean "mighty angels." This seemed to be a problem to the translators of the Septuagint, so they rendered it "lower than angels." Hebrews seems to closely follow the Septuagint; however, the Greek text of Hebrews changes the quotation to read "a little while lower."

b 2:7 This last sentence is missing in some Greek manuscripts; however early and important ones include it, as well as the Aramaic.

c 2:8 Or "you subjected all things under his feet." The command given to both Adam and Eve to "take dominion" (Genesis 1:28) has never been rescinded. The planet will one day be under the rulership of men and women who are under the rulership of Christ.

d 2:9 Implied in the text and made explicit.

e 2:9 A few manuscripts and some external evidence has instead "he, apart from God (separated from God), tasted death." This could be taken to mean that he experienced death only in his humanity and not in his divinity. The Aramaic is "God himself, by his grace, experienced death in the place of every person."

f 2:9 Or "everything," that is, he redeems humanity and restores creation to his original plan.

Jesus Brings Many Sons to Glory

[10]For now he towers above all creation, for all things exist through him and for him.[a] And that God made him, Pioneer[b] of our salvation, perfect through his sufferings, for this is how he brings his many sons and daughters to share in his glory.[c] [11]Jesus, the Holy One, makes us holy. And as sons and daughters, we now belong to his same Father, so he is not ashamed or embarrassed to introduce us as his brothers and sisters![d] [12]For he has said,

> "I will reveal who you really are[e] to my brothers and sisters,
>   and I will glorify you with praises
>   in the midst of the congregation."

[13]And,

> "My confidence rests in God!"[f]

And again he says,

> "Here I am, *one with*[g] the children Yahweh has given me."[h]

[14]Since all his "children" have flesh and blood, so Jesus became human to fully identify with us. He did this, so that he could experience death and annihilate the effects of the intimidating accuser who holds against us the power[i] of death. [15]By embracing death Jesus sets free those who live their entire lives in bondage[j] to the tormenting dread of death. [16]For it is clear

---

a 2:10 The Greek word *prepo* means "to stand out and tower above."

b 2:10 Or "Trailblazer" or "Forerunner." His perfection through sufferings implies that all his sons will come to glorious perfection through hardships. The Aramaic is, "the Prince of Life."

c 2:10 Or "bring many children into his glorious state." Grace gives us the glory that Jesus has. Although it is true that God will not share his glory with another (Isaiah 42:8), but in Christ, we are not "another," we are one with him. See also John 17:22; Romans 8:29–30.

d 2:11 See Song of Songs 4:9–10; 5:1–2.

e 2:12 Or "your name." This quote is taken from Psalm 22:22.

f 2:13 See Psalm 31:14; Isaiah 8:17.

g Implied in the text. Jesus is one with us, his children.

h 2:13 By implication "Here I am, in the midst of the sons and daughters you have given me."

i 2:14 Or "dominion."

j 2:15 Or "slavery."

that he didn't do this for the angels, but for all the sons and daughters of Abraham.[a] [17]This is why he had to be a Man and take hold of our humanity in every way. He made us his brothers and sisters and became our merciful and faithful King-Priest[b] before God; as the One who removed our sins to make us one with him. [18]He suffered and endured every test and temptation, so that he can help us every time we pass through the ordeals of life.[c]

---

a 2:16 See Isaiah 41:8.
b 2:17 The Aramaic can be translated "so that he would be the nurturing Lord of the king-priests."
c 2:18 This chapter gives us the 8 victories Christ won for us at Calvary. 1) He is crowned with glory and honor. 2) He brings many sons into his glory. 3) He is made perfect through his sufferings. 4) We are made holy. 5) By his death he destroyed the Devil, who held the power of death over us. 6) He delivers us completely from the fear of death. 7) He is now our faithful High Priest. 8) He helps us in every temptation.

$$Three$$

Jesus, Greater than Moses

¹And so, dear brothers and sisters, you are now made holy, and each of you is invited to the feast^d of your heavenly calling.^e So fasten your thoughts fully onto Jesus,^f whom we embrace^g as our Apostle and King-Priest.^h ²For he was faithful to the Father who appointed him, in the same way that Moses was a model of faithfulness in what was entrusted to him.ⁱ ³But Jesus is worthy to receive a much greater glory than Moses, for the one who builds a house deserves to be honored more than the house he builds. ⁴Every house is built by someone, but God is the Designer and Builder of all things.

⁵Indeed, Moses served God faithfully in all he gave him to do.^j His

---

d Or "sharers of the feast."

e 3:1 Or "you participate as partners in the heavenly calling." The Greek phrase, "heavenly calling" implies an invitation to a celestial feast. It could also be translated "you are called to share the life of heaven." This calling originates in heaven and draws us into heaven. However, in the Aramaic this phrase is, "called with a calling (from heaven)," which is the Aramaic title of the 3rd book of the Torah, Leviticus, and refers to the calling of the Levites as priests.

f 3:1 Or "you have discovered this Jesus." The Aramaic is, "Jesus, the Messiah."

g 3:1 Or "with whom is our legally binding agreement."

h 3:1 God joins the apostolic and priestly ministries together in Christ. An apostle will always release God's people into their priestly calling of entering into the Holy of Holies without going through a system, a church or a person. The word "King-Priest" is from the Aramaic, which uses a word for a priest not of the Levitical order. Jesus could not be a "High Priest" for he was not born in the tribe of Levi, or a descendant of Aaron, but was of the tribe of Judah. So the word here for priest is not, *cohen*, but the Aramaic word, *kumrea*, the word used for Jethro and Melchizedek. See Genesis 14:18; Exodus 2:16; 3:1; 18:1.

i 3:2 Or "who was faithful in all his house." See Numbers 12:7.

j 3:5 Or "in all God's house."

work prophetically illustrates[a] things that would later be spoken and fulfilled.[b] [6]But Christ is more than a Servant, he was faithful as the Son in charge of God's house. And now we are part of his house if we continue courageously to hold firmly to our bold confidence and our victorious hope.[c]

Secrets from Psalm 95

[7]This is why the Holy Spirit says,[d]

> **"If only you would listen to his voice this day![e]**
> **[8]Don't make him[f] angry by hardening your hearts,**
> **like your ancestors did during the days of their rebellion,[g]**
> **when they were tested in the wilderness.**
> **[9]There your fathers tested me and tried my patience[h]**
> **even though they saw my miracles[i] for forty years**
> **they still doubted me![j]**
> **[10]This ignited my anger with that generation**
> **and I said about them, 'They wander in their hearts**
> **just like they do with their feet,**

---

a 3:5 Or "to testify." The Aramaic is "he believed all the evidence in the house (tabernacle). That is, Moses saw and believed that the tabernacle and all its furnishings were an illustration of something greater that God would unveil later on.

b 3:5 Or "to give testimony to things that would be spoken."

c 3:6 As translated from the Aramaic. The Greek is "the pride (rejoicing) of our hope."

d 3:7 See Psalm 95:7–11. Notice the truth that the Bible is the Holy Spirit of God speaking to us.

e 3:7 The Aramaic is "the echo of his voice." See also v. 15.

f 3:8 As translated from the Aramaic.

g 3:8 The Aramaic could be translated "just like the bitterness at Marah."

h 3:9 This refers to incidents that took place at Massah (testing) and Meribah (strife). See Exodus 17:7; Numbers 20:13. The Septuagint, instead of transliterating those names, translates their meanings and includes them here in the text. A Hebrew reader would have no difficulty in understanding the obvious inference of the rebellion that took place in the desert.

i 3:9 Or "works," however, these works are miracles, when considering the plagues of Egypt, the Passover miracle, the parting of the Red Sea, the manna falling from the sky, water from the rock, etc.

j 3:9 Implied in the context. The Greek is from the Septuagint and is literally "There they tested me by trial." That is, they continually doubted God's faithfulness to them. We must never doubt God, even in a season of difficulty.

and they refuse to learn my ways.'

[11]My heart grieved over them[a] so I decreed:
'They will never enter into the calming rest of my Spirit!'"

[12]So search your hearts every day,[b] my brothers and sisters, and make sure that none of you has evil or unbelief hiding within you. For it will lead you astray,[c] and make you unresponsive to the living God. [13]This is the time to encourage[d] each other to never be stubborn or hardened by sin's deceitfulness.[e] [14]For we are mingled with the Messiah,[f] if we will continue unshaken in this confident assurance[g] from the beginning until the end.

[15]For again, the Scriptures say,[h]

If only today you would listen to his voice.
Don't make him angry[i] by hardening your hearts,
as you did in the wilderness rebellion.

[16]The same people who were delivered from bondage and brought out of Egypt by Moses, were the ones who heard and still rebelled. [17]They grieved God for forty years[j] by sinning in their unbelief, until they dropped dead in the desert. [18]So God swore an oath that they would never enter into his calming place of rest all because they disobeyed him. [19]It is clear that they could not enter into their inheritance[k] because they wrapped their hearts in unbelief.

---

a 3:11 The Greek word *orge* is used for any emotion of extreme passion, usually anger.

b 3:12 As translated from the Aramaic. The Greek is "Take care."

c 3:12 Or "rebel against."

d 3:13 Or "warn."

e 3:13 The Aramaic is "the sin of the deceiver." The deceiver could be referring to the Devil, or to our own ability to be self-deceived.

f 3:14 Or "we are all business partners of Christ." The Aramaic can be translated "We are all sewn (together) with Christ."

g 3:14 The Aramaic can be translated "we are joined (leavened) in the resurrection through him."

h 3:15 See Psalm 95:7–8.

i 3:15 As translated from the Aramaic.

j 3:17 See Numbers 14:33–34.

k 3:19 Implied in the context.

Four

The Faith-Rest Life

[1]Now God has offered to us the same promise of entering into his realm of resting in confident faith. So we must be extremely careful to ensure that we all embrace the fullness of that promise and not fail to experience it. [2]For we have heard the good news of deliverance just as they did, yet they didn't join their faith with the Word[a] and activate its power.[b] Instead, what they heard didn't affect them deeply, for they doubted. [3]For those of us who believe, faith activates the promise and we experience the realm of confident rest! For he has said,[c]

> **"I was grieved[d] with them and made a solemn oath,**
> **'They will never enter into the calming rest of my Spirit.'"**

God's works have all been completed from the foundation of the world,[e] [4]for it says in the Scriptures,[f]

---

a 4:2 Or "because they did not join in with those who heard the message with faith (Joshua and Caleb)."
b 4:2 Implied in the text.
c 4:3 See Psalm 95:11; Hebrews 3:11.
d 4:3 The Greek word *orge* is used for any emotion of extreme passion, usually anger.
e 4:3 Or "God's works have been completed, even though the world has fallen." The Greek word *katabole* means "to fall down, to throw down." It is most often used for "laying down a foundation," but it can imply the fall of humanity through sin. Even though the world has fallen, God's works have already been accomplished, unhindered by the sin of man. God's finished works supersede the brokenness of our planet.
f 4:4 See Genesis 2:2.

And on the seventh day God rested from all his works.

⁵And again, as stated before,

They will never enter into my calming place of rest.

⁶Those who first heard the good news of deliverance failed to enter into that realm of faith's-rest because of their unbelieving hearts. Yet the fact remains that we still have the opportunity to enter into the faith-rest life and experience the fulfillment of the promise! ⁷For God still has ordained a day for us to enter into called "Today." For it was long afterwards that God repeated it in David's words,

> **"If only today you would listen to his voice**
> **and do not harden your hearts!"**

⁸Now if this promise of "rest" was fulfilled when Joshua brought the people into the land,ᵃ God wouldn't have spoken later of another "rest" yet to come. ⁹So we conclude that there is still a full and completeᵇ "rest" waiting for believersᶜ to experience. ¹⁰As we enter into God's faith-rest life we cease from our own works, just as God celebrates his finished works and rests in them.ᵈ ¹¹So then we must give our all and be eager to experience this faith-rest life, so that no one falls short by following the same pattern of doubt and unbelief.

¹²For we have the living Word of God, which is full of energy,ᵉ and it

---

a 4:8 See Joshua 21:44; 22:4.

b 4:9 Or "Sabbath." The Aramaic can be translated "He arose to be the Sabbath for the people of God."

c 4:9 Or "the people of God."

d 4:10 Implied in the text. The word used for "Sabbath" in verse 9 is not the usual word, it is the celebratory aspects of the Sabbath that are emphasized in the Greek word *sabbatismos*.

e 4:12 The Aramaic is "all effective." There is a hint here of the spinning sword of fire, held by the angel guarding the way to the tree of life. To come eat its fruit, you must pass through the mighty sword of fire. The context implies we pass through this "fire-sword" on our way into the Holy of Holies. When the veil was split in two, the cherubim, embroidered on the veil parted, as it were, to allow every worshiper to enter into the unveiled presence of God. See Genesis 3:24; Matthew 27:51.

pierces more sharply than a two-edged sword.[a] It will even penetrate to the very core of our being where soul and spirit, bone[b] and marrow meet![c] It interprets and reveals the true thoughts and secret motives of our hearts. [13]There is not one person who can hide their thoughts from God, for nothing that we do remains a secret, and nothing created is concealed, but everything is exposed and defenseless before his eyes, to whom we must render an account.[d]

Jesus, Our Compassionate King-Priest

[14]So then, we must cling in faith to all we know to be true. For we have a magnificent King-Priest,[e] Jesus Christ, the Son of God, who rose into the heavenly realm for us, and now sympathizes with us in our frailty.[f] [15]He understands humanity, for as a Man, our magnificent King-Priest was tempted in every way just as we are, and conquered sin.[g] [16]So now we come freely and boldly to where love is enthroned,[h] to receive mercy's kiss and discover the grace we urgently need to strengthen[i] us in our time of weakness.[j]

---

a 4:12 Or "than a two-mouthed sword." God speaks his word, then we, in agreement, also speak his word and it becomes a two-mouthed sword.

b 4:12 As translated from the Aramaic, the Greek is "joint."

c 4:12 Soul and spirit are the immaterial parts of every person that make us who we are, joint and bone marrow are the physical aspects of our existence. All of this combined forms our humanity. God's Word has the ability to uncover our hidden aspects and make them known.

d 4:13 The word used here is *logos*. The Greek could also be translated "in his view the Word is our responsibility."

e 4:14 As translated from the Aramaic, which uses a word for a priest not of the Levitical order. The Aramaic word here for priest is not *cohen* but *kumrea*.

f 4:14 The Aramaic is "who has sorrow with us in our affliction."

g 4:15 As translated from the Aramaic. The Greek is "He was without sin (sinless)."

h 4:16 Or "the throne of grace."

i 4:16 The Greek word *boetheia* means "urgent help," and is often used as "reinforcing (a ship in a storm)." See Acts 27:17.

j 4:16 The Aramaic is "tribulation."

Five

___

A King-Priest like Melchizedek

[1]For every High Priest was chosen from among the people and appointed to represent them before God by presenting their gifts to God and offering sacrifices on their behalf. [2]Since the High Priest is also one who is clothed in weakness, he humbles himself[a] by showing compassion to those who are ignorant of God's ways and stray from them. [3]And for this reason, he has to not only present the sin offerings of others, but also to bring a sin offering for himself. [4]And no one takes this honor upon himself by being self-appointed, but God is the one who calls each one, just as Aaron was called.

[5]So also, Christ was not self-appointed and did not glorify himself by becoming a high priest, but God called and glorified him![b] For the Father said to him,

"You are my favored Son. Today I have fathered you."[c]

___

a 5:2 As translated from the Aramaic. There is an alternate translation of the Aramaic which reads "He (Christ) humbled himself and took the sorrows of those who knew nothing and were lost, for he was also clothed in frailty (humanity)."

b 5:5 Apparently, many Jewish believers were having difficulty with Jesus being our High Priest, since he was not of Aaron's lineage from the tribe of Levi. The Holy Spirit is showing us that his priesthood is not on the basis of lineage, but the supernatural calling of God, much like Melchizedek. The meaning of the name Melchizedek is "King of righteousness."

c 5:5 The Aramaic can be translated, "Every day I beget you." See Psalm 2:7, 12; Hebrews 1:5.

⁶And in another Scripture he says about this new priestly order,

"You are a Priest like Melchizedek,[a] a King-Priest forever!"

⁷During Christ's days on earth[b] he pleaded with God, praying with passion and with tearful agony that God would spare him from death.[c] And because of his perfect devotion his prayer was answered and he was delivered. ⁸But even though he was a wonderful Son,[d] he learned to listen[e] and obey through all his sufferings. ⁹And after being proven perfect in this way he has now become the source of eternal salvation to all those who listen to him and obey. ¹⁰For God has designated him as the King-Priest who is over the priestly order of Melchizedek.[f]

Moving On into Full Maturity

¹¹We have much to say about this topic although it is difficult to explain,[g] because you have become too dull and sluggish to understand. ¹²For you should already be professors instructing others by now; but instead, you need to be taught from the beginning the basics of God's prophetic

---

a 5:6 Or "in the succession of Melchizedek." See Psalm 110:4.

b 5:7 Or "During the days when Christ wore flesh."

c 5:7 That is, from a premature death in Gethsemane. The text clearly states that Jesus was spared from death. What death? He gave his life on the cross for us. This seems to reveal that Jesus prayed in the garden to be spared from death that night and live long enough to die on the cross, and not prematurely die in the garden. Most expositors believe this was the "cup" of God's wrath that was the sin payment. Yet it is possible that the "cup" he was asking God to let pass from him was the cup of premature death in the garden, not the death he would experience the next day on the cross. He had already sweat drops of blood, but the prophecies had to be fulfilled of being pierced on a cross for our transgressions. God answered his cry and he lived through the agony of Gethsemane so that he could be our sacrifice for sin on Calvary. Jesus did not waver in the garden. We have a brave Savior! See John 18:11.

d 5:8 As translated from the Aramaic.

e 5:8 The Greek word for obedience *hupakoe* means "to hearken" or "to listen for the knock on the door" or "to pay attention." Also in verse 9. See *Strong's Concordance* 5218 and 5219. Jesus' sufferings were seen as lessons of listening to and obeying God.

f 5:10 As translated from the Aramaic. Jesus, our magnificent King-Priest, has made us kings and priests that serve him and extend his kingdom on the earth. See 1 Peter 2:9–10; Revelation 5:8–10.

g 5:11 The Aramaic is "We have so much more to say about Melchizedek, but his manifestation overwhelms us and makes it difficult to explain."

oracles!*a* You're like children*b* still needing milk and not yet ready to digest solid food. ¹³For every spiritual infant who lives on milk is not yet pierced*c* by the revelation of righteousness.*d* ¹⁴But solid food is for the mature, whose spiritual senses perceive heavenly matters.*e* And they have been adequately trained by what they've experienced to emerge*f* with understanding of the difference between what is truly excellent and what is evil and harmful.

---

a 5:12 Or "the elements of the beginnings of the oracles of God." That is, how Jesus is the substance and fulfillment of the oracles (message) of God.

b 5:12 The Greek word, *nepios* means "still unfit to bear arms," that is, unprepared for battle.

c 5:13 Or "inexperienced." The Greek word *apeiros* means "unpierced." See *Strong's Concordance* 552, 586, 3984, and 4008.

d 5:13 The Aramaic is "they are not unversed in the language (manifestation) of righteousness."

e 5:14 Implied in the text.

f 5:14 As translated from the Aramaic.

$\mathcal{S}ix$

___

Moving On to Deeper Truth

[1]Now is the time for us to progress beyond the basic message of Christ[a] and advance into perfection. The foundation has already been laid for us to build upon: turning away from our dead works[b] to embrace faith in God, [2]teaching about different baptisms,[c] impartation by the laying on of hands,[d] resurrection of the dead, and eternal judgment. [3]So with God's enablement[e] we will move on to deeper truths.

A Warning to Never Turn Away

[4]It is impossible to restore an apostate.[f] For once a person has come into God's light,[g] and tasted the gifts of the heavenly realm, and has received the Holy Spirit,[h] [5]and feasted on the good Word of God, and has entered into the power of the age that is breaking in,[i] [6]if he abandons his faith, there

___

a 6:1 Or "the Word (*Logos*) of the beginning of Christ."

b 6:1 Or "useless deeds." *Dead works* are the attempts of people to please God through religion, keeping religious laws and traditions, and serving others to gain influence with God. There was one "work" that brings life to all, that was the "work" of Christ on the cross.

c 6:2 The New Testament speaks of seven baptisms, including the baptism of fire, the baptism of the Holy Spirit, the baptism of suffering (Jesus' cross), the baptism into the cloud, the baptism into Moses, the baptism of repentance, and water baptism.

d 6:2 This was done in the Old and New Testaments to heal, to bless others, to impart the Holy Spirit and his gifts, to identify with a person (or sacrifice), and to release others to their calling and ministry.

e 6:3 Or "If God entrusts it to us." The Aramaic uses here the title for God "the Lord YHWH."

f 6:4 That is, one who has abandoned their faith. Because of the extraordinary length of the Greek sentence, this summary statement implied in the text is given here at the beginning of the paragraph for the sake of English narrative. To say it is impossible does not mean that God cannot bring them to repentance, but that he chooses to leave them in their hardened state, much like Pharaoh who hardened his heart to God. The Aramaic is very clear, "they cannot be renewed to conversion."

g 6:4 The Aramaic is "they have descended once into baptism."

h 6:4 Or "has been in (business) partnership with the Holy Spirit."

i 6:5 Or "the age that is about to come."

is no use even trying to lead him to repentance. By their sin of apostasy[a] they re-crucify the Son of God,[b] and have publicly repudiated him.[c]

[7]For men's hearts[d] are just like the soil that drinks up the showers which often fall upon it. Some soil will yield crops as God's blessing upon the field. [8]But if the field continues to produce only thorns and thistles[e] a curse hangs over it and will be burned.

[9]Having said that, beloved, we are fully convinced that there are more beautiful and excellent things, which flow from your salvation.[f]

[10]For God, the Faithful One, is not unfair.[g] How can he forget[h] the work you have done for him? He remembers the love you demonstrate as you continually serve[i] his beloved ones[j] for the glory of his name. [11]But we long to see you passionately advance until the end and you find your hope fulfilled. [12]So don't allow your hearts to grow dull[k] or lose your enthusiasm, but follow the example of those who fully received what God has promised[l] because of their strong faith and patient endurance.[m]

God's Faithful Promise

[13]Now when God made a promise to Abraham, since there was no one greater than himself, he swore an oath on his own integrity[n] to keep the promise as sure as God exists! [14]So he said,

---

a 6:6 As translated from the Aramaic and implied in the Greek.

b 6:6 Or "it is impossible to crucify the Son of God again for them to change their own minds!"

c 6:6 Or "have made a public spectacle of him." The Aramaic is "insulted the Son of God."

d 6:7 Implied in the text and supplied for the sake of English narrative.

e 6:8 These are the consequences of sin from the time of Adam. See Genesis 3:18.

f 6:9 Or "things which cling to salvation."

g 6:10 The Aramaic is "God is not evil."

h 6:10 He won't remember our sins, but will remember our works of loving service to others.

i 6:10 The Greek text implies financially providing for others.

j 6:10 Or "saints (holy ones)."

k 6:12 The Greek word for "dull of heart" is *nothros*, which is taken from a root word meaning "illegitimate child." The implication is that we don't see ourselves as a child of illegitimacy, but a child of intimacy that keeps our relationship fervent and passionate.

l 6:12 The Aramaic is "to those who were heirs of the royal proclamation."

m 6:12 The Aramaic is "because of their faith and the outpouring of the Spirit."

n 6:13 See Genesis 22:16–17.

**"Have no doubt, I promise to bless you over and over,
and give you a son**^a **and multiply you without measure!"**

¹⁵So Abraham waited patiently in faith and succeeded in seeing the promise fulfilled.^b ¹⁶It is very common for people to swear an oath by something greater than themselves, for the oath will confirm their statements and end all dispute. ¹⁷So in the same way, God wanted to end all doubt and confirm it even more forcefully to those who would inherit his promises. His purpose was unchangeable, so God added his vow to the promise. ¹⁸So it is impossible for God to lie for we know that his promise and his vow will never change!

And now we have run into his heart to hide ourselves in his faithfulness. This is where we find his strength and comfort, for he empowers us to seize what has already been established ahead of time—an unshakeable hope! ¹⁹We have this certain hope like a strong, unbreakable anchor holding our souls to God himself. Our anchor of hope is fastened to the mercy seat^c which sits in the heavenly realm beyond the sacred threshold,^d ²⁰and where Jesus, our Forerunner,^e has gone in before us. He is now and forever our Royal Priest like Melchizedek.^f

---

a 6:14 Implied in the text.

b 6:15 That is, through the birth of Isaac. The Aramaic is fascinating, for the name of Abraham is not in the Greek text in this verse: "And he (God) bestowed his Spirit and he (Abraham) received the kingdom."

c 6:19 Implied in the text and made explicit as that which is found inside the innermost chamber.

d 6:19 As translated from the Aramaic, which is literally "beyond the faces of the door."

e 6:20 Or "Trailblazer." Jesus has blazed a trail for us to enter into the sacred chamber and seize the hope that has been fulfilled in his eyes already, to have a company of king-priests who will dwell with him in the Holiest of Holies and minister from there out to the nations of the earth. The clear implication of verses 19–20 is that he takes us in to share his throne and his ministry as the Royal Priest.

f 6:20 Or "in the order (likeness) of Melchizedek."

$\mathcal{Seven}$

The Melchizedek Priesthood

1-2Melchizedek's name means "king of righteousness." He was the King of Peace, because the name of the city he ruled as king was Salem, which means "peace." And he was also a priest of the Most High God. Now when Abraham was returning from defeating many kings in battle, Melchizedek went out to meet him and blessed him. Then Abraham took a tenth of everything he had won in battle and gave it to Melchizedek.[a] 3This Melchizedek has no father or mother, and no record of any of his ancestors. He was never born and he never died, but his life is like a picture[b] of the Son of God, a King-Priest forever! 4Now let me show you proof of how great this Melchizedek is:

- Even though Abraham was the most honored and favored patriarch of all God's chosen ones,[c] he gave a tithe of the spoils of battle to Melchizedek. 5It would be understandable if Melchizedek had been a Jewish priest, for later on God's people were required by law to support their priests financially, because the priests were their relatives and Abraham's descendants. 6But Melchizedek was not Abraham's Jewish relative,[d] and yet Abraham still paid him a tithe.

---

a 7:1-2 See Genesis 14:17-20.
b 7:3 Or "made to resemble."
c 7:4 Implied in the text with the comparison made explicit.
d 7:6 Or "does not share their ancestry."

- Melchizedek imparted a blessing on mighty Abraham, who had received the promises of God. ⁷And no one could deny the fact that the one who has the power to impart a blessing is superior to the one who receives it.
- ⁸Although the Jewish priests received tithes, they all died—they were mortal. But Melchizedek lives on!
- ⁹It could even be said that Levi, the ancestor of every Jewish priest who received tithes, actually paid tithes to Melchizedek through Abraham. ¹⁰For although Levi was yet unborn, the seed from which Levi came was present in Abraham[a] when he paid his tithe to Melchizedek.
- ¹¹If any of the Levitical priests who served under the law had the power to bring us into perfection, then why did God send Christ as Priest after the likeness of Melchizedek? He should have said, "After the likeness of Aaron."
- ¹²And furthermore, for God to send a new and different rank of priest, meant a new law would have had to be instituted even to allow it!

Jesus and the Priesthood of Melchizedek

¹³Yet the One these things all point to, was from a different tribe and no one from that tribe ever officiated at God's altar, ¹⁴for we all know that our Lord didn't descend from the tribe of Levi, but shined from the tribe of Judah.[b] And Moses himself never said anything of a priest in connection with Judah's tribe.

¹⁵And all this is made even clearer if there was another King-Priest raised up with the rank of Melchizedek. ¹⁶This King-Priest did not arise

---

a 7:10 Or "Levi was in the loins of his father, Abraham." In effect, Abraham submitted all his sons to the priesthood of Melchizedek.

b 7:14 As translated from the Aramaic.

because of a genealogical right under the law to be a priest, but by the power of an indestructible, resurrection life![a]

[17]For it says in the Psalms,

You are like Melchizedek, a King-Priest forever!

[18]The old order of priesthood[b] has been set aside as weak and powerless.[c] [19]For the law[d] has never made anyone perfect, but in its place is a far better hope which gives us confidence to experience intimacy with God! [20]And he confirmed it to us with his solemn vow.[e] For the former priests took their office without an oath, [21]but with Jesus, God affirmed his royal-priesthood with his promise, saying,

The Lord has made a solemn oath
  and will never change his mind,
  "You are a King-Priest forever!"[f]

[22]So all of this magnifies the truth that we have a superior covenant with God than what they experienced, for Jesus himself is its Guarantor![g] [23]As additional proof, we know there were many priests under the old system, for they eventually died and their office had to be filled by another. [24]But Jesus permanently holds his priestly office, since he lives forever and will never have a successor![h]

[25]So he is able to save fully from now throughout eternity,[i] everyone

---

a 7:15 The word *indestructible* comes from a word that means, "tied together in unity," that is, "a united life (union with God)." Resurrection life is implied, for the priestly ministry of Jesus began after he was raised from the dead. The Aramaic is "He has life-giving power that has no beginning." Jesus' ministry of Prophet, Priest, and King flows from his unlimited life of resurrection power!

b 7:18 Implied in the context.

c 7:18 Or "useless."

d 7:19 Or in Aramaic "Torah."

e 7:20 As translated from the Aramaic. The Greek is "Since this was not done with a solemn oath, for the others became priests without a sworn oath."

f 7:21 See Psalm 110:4; Hebrews 5:6; 6:20; 7:17.

g 7:22 The Aramaic can be translated "through which we gained Jesus."

h 7:24 As translated from the Aramaic and implied in the Greek.

i 7:25 The Greek text is somewhat ambiguous, an alternative translation could be "He is able to save who comes to God through him, because he lives to pray continually for them. ²⁶He is the High Priest who perfectly fits our need—holy, without a trace of evil, without the ability to deceive, incapable of sin,ᵃ and exalted beyond the heavens!

²⁷Unlike the former high priests, he is not compelled to offer daily sacrifices. They had to bring a sacrifice first for their own sins,ᵇ then for the sins of the people, but he finished the sacrificial system, once and for all, when he offered himself. ²⁸The law appointed flawed men as high priests, but God's promise, sealed with his oath, which succeeded the law, appoints a perfect Son who is complete forever!

---

for all time" or "He is able, now and always, to completely (fully) save."
a   7:26 As translated from the Aramaic. The Greek is "separate from sinners."
b   7:27 See Leviticus 16:6–16.

Eight

Our Better Covenant

¹Now this is the crowning point of what we are saying: We have a magnificent King-Priest who ministers for us at the right hand of God. He is enthroned with honor next to the throne of the Majesty on high. ²He serves in the holy sanctuary in the true heavenly tabernacle[a] set up by God, and not by men. ³Since every high priest is appointed to offer both gifts and sacrifices, so the Messiah also had to bring some sacrifice. ⁴But since he didn't qualify to be an earthly priest, and there are already priests who offer sacrifices[b] prescribed by the law, he offered in heaven a perfect sacrifice.[c]

⁵The priests on earth serve in a temple that is but a copy modeled after the heavenly sanctuary; a shadow of the reality. For when Moses began to construct the tabernacle God warned him and said,

> **"You must precisely follow the pattern I revealed to you on Mt. Sinai."**[d]

---

a 8:2 Or "tent."

b 8:4 Or "gifts." The present tense of the verb used here shows that there was still a temple with sacrifices being offered at the time of writing Hebrews. This sets the date as before 70 AD when the temple was destroyed by the Roman war.

c 8:4 This clause is implied and made explicit for the sake of clarity.

d 8:5 Implied in the text. See also Exodus 25:40.

⁶But now Jesus the Messiah[a] has accepted a priestly ministry which far surpasses theirs, since he is the Catalyst[b] of a better covenant which contains far more wonderful promises! ⁷For if that first covenant had been faultless no one would have needed a second one to replace it. ⁸But God revealed the defect and limitation of the first when he said to his people,[c]

> "Look! The day will come, declares the Lord,
>> when I will satisfy the people of Israel and Judah
>> by giving them a new covenant.[d]
> ⁹It will be an entirely different covenant
>> than the one I made with their fathers
>> when I led them by my hand out of Egypt.
>> For they did not remain faithful to my covenant,
>> so I rejected them, says the Lord God.
> ¹⁰For here is the covenant I will one day establish
>> with the people of Israel:
>> I will embed my laws within their thoughts
>> and fasten them onto their hearts.
>> I will be their loyal God and they will be my loyal people.
> ¹¹And the result of this will be[e]
>> that everyone will know me as Lord!
>> There will be no need at all
>> to teach their fellow-citizens or brothers by saying,
>> 'You should know the Lord Jehovah,'
>> since everyone will know me inwardly,[f]

---

a 8:6 As translated from the Aramaic. The Greek is simply "he."
b 8:6 As translated from the Aramaic. The Greek is "the covenant that he mediates (as Intermediary and Guarantor)."
c 8:8 Some Greek manuscripts have "Because he found fault with them (Israelites)."
d 8:8 As translated from the Aramaic. The Greek is "I will complete a new covenant with the house of Israel and the house of Judah."
e 8:11 Implied in the text and supplied for clarity.
f 8:11 Implied in the context.

> from the most unlikely
>   to the most distinguished.[a]
> 12For I will demonstrate my mercy to them
>   and will forgive[b] their evil deeds,
>   and never remember again their sins."

13This proves that by establishing this new covenant the first is now obsolete, ready to expire, and about to disappear.[c]

---

a 8:11 The Aramaic is "from the youngest to the oldest."
b 8:12 The Aramaic is "I will make atonement for their evil."
c 8:13 Or "is near obliteration." The *old* which is *about to disappear,* can also refer to our *old* life and its *old* ways of pleasing flesh; the sinful disposition of our hearts. The Aramaic verb for *disappear* can also mean "to give birth."

$\mathcal{N}ine$

___

The Old Pattern of Worship

[1]Now in the first covenant there were specific rules for worship including a sanctuary on earth to worship in. [2]When you entered the tabernacle you would first come into the holy chamber where you would find the lampstand[a] and the bread of his presence on the fellowship table.[b] [3]Then as you pass through the next curtain[c] you would enter the innermost chamber called, the Holiest Sanctuary of All.[d] [4]It contained the golden altar of incense and the ark of covenant mercy, which was a wooden box covered entirely with gold. And placed inside the ark of covenant mercy was the golden jar with mystery-manna inside,[e] Aaron's resurrection rod, which had sprouted, and the stone tablets engraved with the covenant laws. [5]On top of the lid of the ark were two cherubim, angels of splendor, with outstretched wings overshadowing the throne of mercy.[f] But now is not the time to discuss further the significant details of these things.

[6]So with this prescribed pattern of worship the priests would routinely go in and out of the first chamber to perform their religious duties. [7]And the high priest was permitted to enter into the Holiest Sanctuary of All only

---

a 9:2 See Exodus 25:31–40; Leviticus 24:1–4.
b 9:2 See Exodus 25:23–30; 39:36. This fellowship table had 12 loaves of sacred bread. See also Leviticus 24:5–9.
c 9:3 See Exodus 26:31–35.
d 9:3 Or "Holy of Holies," that is, the Holiest Place of All.
e 9:4 The Hebrew word for manna, the wilderness bread, means "mystery" or "What is it?"
f 9:5 Or "the place of atonement." See Exodus 25:18–22.

once a year and he could never enter without first offering sacrificial blood for both his own sins and for the sins of the people.

[8]Now the Holy Spirit uses the symbols of this pattern of worship to reveal that the perfect way of holiness[a] had not yet been unveiled. For as long as the tabernacle stood [9]it was an illustration[b] that pointed to our present time of fulfillment,[c] demonstrating that offerings and animal sacrifices had failed to perfectly cleanse the conscience of the worshiper. [10]For this old pattern of worship was a matter of external rules and rituals concerning food and drink and ceremonial washings which was imposed upon us until the appointed time of heart-restoration had arrived.[d]

The Heavenly Pattern of Worship

[11]But now the Anointed One has become the King-Priest of every wonderful thing that has come.[e] For he serves in a greater, more perfect heavenly tabernacle[f] not made by men. [12]And he has entered once and forever into the Holiest Sanctuary of All, not with the blood of animal sacrifices, but the sacred blood of his own sacrifice. And he alone has made our salvation[g] secure forever!

[13]Under the old covenant the blood of bulls, goats, and the ashes of a heifer were sprinkled on those who were defiled and effectively cleansed them outwardly from their ceremonial impurities. [14]Yet how much more will the sacred blood of the Messiah thoroughly cleanse our consciences! For by the power of the eternal Spirit he has offered himself to God as the

---

a 9:8 As translated from the Aramaic. The Greek is "the way into the Holy Place."

b 9:9 The Aramaic is "mystery."

c 9:9 Implied in the context.

d 9:10, The Greek word *diothosis* is used only here in the New Testament. It means to set things right, or to snap a broken bone back into place, by implication *restoration*.

e 9:11 The Aramaic is "the good things that he did." Some Greek manuscripts have, "good things that are coming."

f 9:11 Or "not of this creation (world)."

g 9:12 Or "He has paid the ransom (redemption) forever."

perfect[a] Sacrifice that now frees[b] us from our dead works[c] to worship and serve the living God.

[15]So Jesus is the One who has enacted a new covenant with a new relationship with God so that those who accept the invitation[d] will receive the eternal inheritance he has promised to his heirs. For he died to release us from the guilt of the violations committed under the first covenant.

[16-17]Now a person's last will and testament can only take effect after one has been proven to have died; otherwise the will cannot be in force while the person who made it is still alive. [18]So this is why not even the first covenant was inaugurated without the blood of animals. [19]For Moses ratified the covenant after he gave the people all the commandments of the law. He took the blood of calves and goats, with water, scarlet wool, and a hyssop branch, and sprinkled both the people and the book of the covenant,[e] [20]saying,

> **"This is the blood of the covenant that God commands you to keep."**[f]

[21]And later Moses also sprinkled the tabernacle with blood and every utensil and item used in their service of worship. [22]Actually, nearly everything under the law was purified with blood, since forgiveness only comes through an outpouring of blood.

[23]And so it was necessary for all the earthly symbols[g] of the heavenly realities to be purified with these animal sacrifices, but the heavenly things themselves required a superior sacrifice than these. [24]For the Messiah did

---

a 9:14 Or "unblemished."

b 9:14 Or "purifies."

c 9:14 Or "what we did when we were corpses."

d 9:15 Or "those who are called."

e 9:19 See Exodus 24:3, 7.

f 9:20 See Exodus 24:8. The blood of Jesus gave birth to the new covenant for the forgiveness of sins. See Matthew 26:28.

g 9:23 Or "outlines" or "sketches."

not enter into the earthly tabernacle made by men, which was but an echo of the true sanctuary, but he entered into heaven itself to appear before the face[a] of God in our place. [25]Under the old system year after year the high priest entered the most holy sanctuary with blood that was not his own. But the Messiah did not need to repeatedly offer himself year after year, [26]for that would mean he must suffer repeatedly ever since the fall of the world.[b] But now he has appeared at the fulfillment of the ages to abolish[c] sin once and for all by the sacrifice of himself!

[27]Every human being is appointed to die once, and then to face God's judgment.[d] [28]But when we die we will be face-to-face with Christ,[e] the One who once experienced death once for all to bear the sins of many![f] And now we eagerly expect to see him in a second appearing; not to bear our sins, but to bring us the fullness of salvation.[g]

---

a 9:24 As translated from the Aramaic (Hebrew), which has no word equivalent for "presence," only face. To come into God's presence meant that you come before his face.

b 9:26 Or "from the foundation of the world." The Greek word *katabole* can also mean "laying down" or "falling down (of the world through sin)," which by implication means *Adam's sin.*

c 9:26 The Aramaic is "annihilate sin."

d 9:27 The Greek is literally "a court trial."

e 9:28 Implied in the context.

f 9:28 The Aramaic is "to burn away (obliterate) the sins of many." See Isaiah 53:12.

g 9:28 There is a salvation that is yet to be unveiled. See 1 Peter 1:5.

Ten

Christ's Eternal Sacrifice

[1]The old system of living under the law presented us with only a faint shadow, a crude outline of the reality of the wonderful blessings to come. Even with its steady stream of sacrifices offered year after year, there still was nothing that could make our hearts perfect before God. [2-3]For if animal sacrifices could once and for all eliminate sin, they would have ceased to be offered and the worshipers would have clean consciences. Instead, once was not enough so by the repetitive sacrifices year after year, the worshipers were continually reminded of their sins, with their hearts still impure. [4]For what power does the blood of bulls and goats[a] have to remove sin's guilt?

[5]So when Jesus the Messiah came into the world he said,

> **"Since your ultimate desire was not another animal sacrifice,**
> **you have clothed me with a body**[b]
> **that I might offer myself instead!**
> [6]**Multiple burnt offerings and sin-offerings**
> **cannot satisfy your justice.**
> [7]**So I said to you, 'God—**

---

a 10:4 The Aramaic is "bulls and birds."

b 10:5 As translated from the Aramaic. See also Psalm 40:6-8. The Hebrew of Psalm 40:6 has, "My ears you have pierced." The Clementine Septuagint has "My ears you have prepared."

> I will be the One to go and do your will,
> to fulfill all that is written of me in your Word!'"[a]

[8]First he said, "Multiple burnt-offerings and sin-offerings cannot satisfy your justice" (even though the law required them to be offered).

[9]And then he said, "God, I will be the One to go and do your will." So by being the sacrifice that removes sin,[b] he abolishes animal sacrifices[c] and replaces that entire system with the new covenant.[d] [10]By God's will we have been purified and made holy once and for all[e] through the sacrifice of the body of Jesus, the Messiah!

[11]Yet every day priests still serve, ritually offering the same sacrifices again and again— sacrifices that can never take away sin's guilt. [12]But when this Priest had offered the one supreme sacrifice for sin for all time he sat down on a throne at the right hand of God, [13]waiting until all his whispering enemies are subdued and turn into his footstool. [14]And by his one perfect sacrifice he made us perfectly holy[f] and complete for all time!

[15]The Holy Spirit confirms this to us by this Scripture, for the Lord says,

> [16]"Afterwards, I will give them this covenant: I will embed my laws into their hearts and fasten my Word to their thoughts."

[17]And then he says,

> "I will not ever again remember their sins and lawless deeds!"[g]

---

a 10:7 Or "in the scroll of the Book." The Aramaic is "from the beginning of your writings (the Torah) it is spoken of me."

b 10:9 Implied in the text and added to clarify the English narrative.

c 10:9 Implied in the context.

d 10:9 Or "the second (covenant)."

e 10:10 Or "made holy through the offering up of the body of Jesus Christ once and for all."

f Or "we are being made holy."

g 10:17 See Jeremiah 31:33–34.

¹⁸So if our sins have been forgiven and forgotten, why would we ever need to offer another sacrifice for sin?

Our Confidence before God

¹⁹And now we are brothers and sisters in God's family because of the blood of Jesus, and he welcomes us to come right into the most holy sanctuary in the heavenly realm—boldly and with no hesitation. ²⁰For he has dedicated a new,[a] life-giving way for us to approach God. For just as the veil was torn in two, Jesus' body was torn open to give us free and fresh access to him!

²¹And since we now have a magnificent King-Priest to welcome us into God's house, ²²we come closer to God and approach him[b] with an open heart, fully convinced by faith that nothing will keep us at a distance from him. For our hearts have been sprinkled with blood to remove impurity and we have been freed from an accusing conscience and now we are clean, unstained, and presentable to God inside and out![c]

²³So now we must cling tightly to the hope that lives within us, knowing that God always keeps his promises![d] ²⁴Discover creative ways to encourage others[e] and to motivate them toward acts of compassion, doing beautiful works as expressions of love. ²⁵This is not the time to to pull away and neglect[f] meeting together, as some have formed the habit of doing, because we need each other! In fact, we should come together even more frequently, eager to encourage and urge each other onward as we anticipate that day dawning.

---

a 10:20 Or "newly slain."
b Or "Draw near to God," or "Offer a true sacrifice. The Hebrew verb "to draw near" (lehitkarev) and to offer a sacrifice (lehakriv) is nearly identical and both are taken from the same root word.
c 10:22 Or "our bodies washed with pure water."
d 10:23 The Aramaic is "Faithful is the One who sent us this message of hope."
e 10:24 The Aramaic is "Let us look on one another with the excitement of love."
f 10:25 Or "abandon." The Greek implies a person who is extremely discouraged.

Another Warning

²⁶For if we continue to persist in deliberate sin after we have known and received the truth, there is not another sacrifice for sin to be made for us. ²⁷But this would qualify one for the certain, terrifying expectation of judgment and the raging fire ready to burn up his enemies!ᵃ ²⁸Anyone who disobeyed Moses' law died without mercy on the simple evidence of two or three witnesses. ²⁹How much more severely do you suppose a person deserves to be judged who has contempt for God's Son,ᵇ and who scorns the blood of the new covenant that made him holy, and who mocks the Spirit who gives him grace?

³⁰For we know him who said,

> **"I have the right to take revenge**
> **and pay them back for their evil!"**

And also,

> **"The Lord God will judge his own people!"**ᶜ

³¹It is the most terrifying thing of all to come under the judgmentᵈ of the Living God!

³²Don't you remember those days right after the Light shined in your hearts?ᵉ You endured a great marathon season of suffering hardships, yet you stood your ground. ³³And at times you were publicly and shamefully mistreated, being persecuted for your faith;ᶠ then at others times you stood side by side with those who preach the message of hope.ᵍ

---

a 10:27 See Isaiah 26:11.
b 10:29 Or "who tramples the Son of God under his feet."
c 10:30 See Deuteronomy 32:35–36.
d 10:31 Or "to fall into the hands."
e 10:32 The Aramaic is "after you were baptized."
f 10:33 The Aramaic is "so that you would become seers" or "develop vision."
g 10:33 As translated from the Aramaic. The Greek is "partners with those who were similarly abused."

³⁴You sympathized with those in prison[a] and when all your belongings were confiscated you accepted that violation with joy; convinced that you possess a treasure growing in heaven[b] that could never be taken from you. ³⁵So don't lose your bold, courageous faith, for you are destined for a great reward![c]

³⁶You need the strength of endurance to reveal the poetry[d] of God's will and then you receive the promise in full. ³⁷For soon and very soon,

"The One who is appearing will come without delay!"[e]

³⁸And he also says,[f]

"My righteous ones will live from my faith.[g]
But if fear holds them back,[h]
my soul is not content with them!"

³⁹But we are certainly not those who are held back by fear and perish; we are among those who have faith and experience true life![i]

---

a 10:34 Or "my (Paul) imprisonment."
b 10:34 As translated from the Aramaic. The Greek is "you possess greater heavenly things."
c 10:35 As translated from the Aramaic. The Greek is "your faith yields a great reward."
d 10:36 Or "to do God's will." The Greek word for "do" is taken from the Greek word *poeima* (poem or poetry).
e 10:37 That is, time is not relevant in the realm of the Spirit. Isaiah 26:20; Habakkuk 2:3–4.
f 10:38 Supplied for clarity of the English narrative.
g 10:38 As translated from the Aramaic, and the Septuagint of Habakkuk 2:4.
h 10:38 The Greek word *hupostello* (aroist subjunctive middle used absolutely), does not mean "to draw back" but "to cower in fear."
i 10:39 Or "faith to the preservation of the soul." The Aramaic is "faith that fulfills our soul."

Eleven

The Power of Bold Faith

[1]Now faith brings our hopes into reality and becomes the foundation needed to acquire the things we long for. It is all the evidence required to prove what is still unseen. [2]This testimony of faith is what previous generations[a] were commended for. [3]Faith empowers us to see that the universe was created and beautifully coordinated[b] by the power of God's words! He spoke and the invisible realm gave birth to all that is seen.

[4]Faith moved Abel[c] to choose a more acceptable sacrifice to offer God than his brother Cain, and God declared him righteous because of his offering of faith. By his faith, Abel still speaks instruction to us today, even though he is long dead.

[5]Faith lifted Enoch from this life and he was taken up into heaven! He never had to experience death; he just disappeared from this world because God promoted him. For before he was translated to the heavenly realm his life had become a pleasure to God.[d]

[6]And without faith living within us it would be impossible to please God.[e] For we come to God in faith[f] knowing that he is real and that he

---

a 11:2 Or "elders."

b 11:3 Or "the ages were completely equipped."

c Although Abel is the subject of the Greek sentence, faith is the emphasis and focus of this chapter. Nothing would have been accomplished by the figures mentioned in verse 4–29 without faith. It is assumed that it is the faith of the person mentioned, not merely an abstraction of faith.

d 11:5 Or "he had the reputation of pleasing God." See Genesis 5:24.

e 11:6 Or "we are powerless to please God." The Greek word *adynatos* means impotent or powerless.

f 11:6 Or "Anyone who approaches God must believe."

rewards the faith of those who give all their passion and strength into seeking him.

[7]Faith opened Noah's heart to receive revelation and warnings from God about what was coming, even things that had never been seen. But he stepped out in reverent obedience to God and built an ark that would save him and his family. By his faith the world was condemned, but Noah received God's gift of righteousness that comes by believing.

Faith of the Patriarchs

[8]Faith motivated Abraham to obey God's call and leave the familiar to discover the territory he was destined to inherit from God. So he left with only a promise and without even knowing ahead of time where he was going, Abraham stepped out in faith. [9]He lived by faith as an immigrant in his promised land as though it belonged to someone else.[a] He journeyed through the land living in tents with Isaac and Jacob who were persuaded that they were also co-heirs of the same promise.

[10]His eyes of faith were set on[b] the city with unshakable foundations, whose architect and builder is God himself. [11]Sarah's faith embraced the miracle power to conceive even though she was barren and was past the age of childbearing, for the authority of her faith[c] rested in the One who made the promise, and she tapped into his faithfulness.

[12]In fact, so many children were subsequently fathered by this aged man of faith—one who was as good as dead, that he now has offspring as innumerable as the sand on the seashore and as the stars in the sky!

[13]These heroes all died still clinging to their faith, not even receiving all that had been promised them. But they saw beyond the horizon the

---

a 11:9 Or "a foreign country."
b 11:10 Or "He was continually receiving the city."
c 11:11 As translated from the Aramaic and some Greek manuscripts. Arguably, a difficult passage to translate from the Greek, variations of the text are focused on Abraham's faith, not Sarah's. Other manuscripts seem to have the focus on "their faith (both Sarah and Abraham)."

fulfillment of their promises and gladly embraced it from afar. They all lived their lives on earth as those who belonged to another realm.[a]

[14]For clearly, those who live this way[b] are longing for the appearing of a heavenly city.[c] [15]And if their hearts were still remembering what they left behind, they would have found an opportunity to go back. [16]But they couldn't turn back for their hearts were fixed on what was far greater, that is, the heavenly realm![d]

So because of this God is not ashamed in any way to be called their God, for he has prepared a heavenly city for them.

Abraham, Isaac, and Jacob

[17]Faith operated powerfully in Abraham for when he was put to the test he offered up Isaac. Even though he received God's promises[e] of descendants, he was willing[f] to offer up his only son! [18]For God had promised,

> **"Through your son Isaac your lineage will carry on your name."**[g]

[19]Abraham's faith made it logical to him that God could raise Isaac from the dead, and symbolically,[h] that's exactly what happened.

[20]The power of faith prompted Isaac to impart a blessing to his sons, Jacob and Esau, concerning their prophetic destinies.

[21]Jacob worshiped in faith's reality at the end of his life, and leaning upon his staff he imparted a prophetic blessing upon each of Joseph's sons.[i]

---

a 11:13 Or "as strangers and nomads on earth."
b 11:14 Or "speak this way."
c 11:14 As translated from the Aramaic. The Greek is "homeland (country)."
d 11:16 It should be noted that there is no mention of "land" or "country" in the Greek text of verses 15–16.
e 11:17 The Aramaic is "he received the royal-proclamation," the Aramaic word for *promise*.
f 11:17 Or "he attempted to offer up."
g 11:18 Or "in Isaac seed will be named for you." See Genesis 21:12.
h 11:19 Or "Isaac was given to him as a parable."
i 11:21 See Genesis 49.

²²Faith inspired Joseph and opened his eyes to see into the future, for as he was dying he prophesied about the exodus*a* of Israel out of Egypt,*b* and gave instructions that his bones were to be taken from Egypt with them.*c*

Moses

²³Faith prompted the parents of Moses at his birth to hide him for three months,*d* because they realized their child was exceptional*e* and refused to be afraid of the king's edict.

²⁴Faith enabled Moses to choose God's will, for although he was raised as the son of Pharaoh's daughter, he refused to make that his identity, ²⁵choosing instead to suffer mistreatment with the people of God. Moses preferred faith's certainty above the momentary enjoyment of sin's pleasures. ²⁶He found his true wealth in suffering abuse for being anointed,*f* more than in anything the world could offer him,*g* for his eyes looked with wonder not on the immediate, but on the ultimate—faith's great reward!*h* ²⁷Holding faith's promise Moses abandoned Egypt and had no fear of Pharaoh's rage because he persisted in faith as if he had seen God who is unseen.*i*

---

a 11:22 Or "remembering the exodus." This is amazing, since the exodus had not yet happened, so how could Joseph "remember" it? This is the eye of faith that imparts prophetic vision of the future.

b 11:22 See Genesis 50:24–25.

c 11:22 See Genesis 47:29–30.

d 11:23 See Exodus 2:2.

e 11:23 Or "elegant." This can mean pleasing in appearance and/or good character.

f 11:26 Or "the reproach of Christ." The Greek text can be translated with either Moses as the one anointed, or Christ, the Anointed One. Moses saw the messianic hope and esteemed it greater than momentary affliction. He believed in the coming Anointed One and held the promise dear.

g 11:26 Or "the storehouses of Egypt."

h 11:26 The Aramaic is "he was paid back in the reward of a Messiah!"

i 11:27 As translated from the Aramaic. The Greek does not have "God" but can be translated "Moses was patient for the invisible as though he were able to see it come to be."

²⁸Faith stirred Moses to perform*ᵃ* the rite of Passover and sprinkle lamb's blood,*ᵇ* to prevent the destroyer from harming their firstborn.*ᶜ*

²⁹Faith opened the way for the Hebrews to cross the Red Sea as if on dry land, but when the Egyptians tried to cross they were swallowed up and drowned!

Jericho and Rahab

³⁰Faith pulled down Jericho's walls after the people marched around them for seven days!

³¹Faith provided a way of escape for Rahab the prostitute, avoiding the destruction of the unbelievers, because she received the Hebrew spies in peace.

More Faith Champions

³²And what more could I say to convince you? For there is not enough time to tell you of the faith of Gideon, Barak, Samson, Jephthah, David, Samuel, and the prophets. ³³Through faith's power they conquered kingdoms and established true justice. Their faith fastened onto their promises and pulled them into reality! It was faith that shut the mouth of lions, ³⁴put out the power of raging fire, and caused many to escape certain death by the sword. In their weakness their faith imparted power to make them strong!*ᵈ* Faith sparked courage within them and they became mighty warriors in battle, pulling armies from another realm into battle array.*ᵉ* ³⁵Faith-filled women saw their dead children raised in resurrection power.

---

a 11:28 This is the perfect tense of the Greek, implying that the Passover is still observed.
b 11:28 Or "pouring out of (lamb's) blood."
c 11:28 That is, "firstborn people and animals."
d 11:34 The Aramaic is "They were restored (healed) from sickness."
e 11:34 See Judges 7 and 16:19–30. Although most translate this "causing enemy armies to flee" the Greek is literally "wheeling ranks drawn up in battle order, ranks which belonged to another." The implication is that through their faith, angelic warriors *wheeled* into battle formation ready to fight with them in battle.

Yet it was faith that enabled others to endure great atrocities. They were stretched out on the wheel and tortured,[a] and didn't deny their faith in order to be freed, because they longed for a more honorable and glorious resurrection!

[36]Others were mocked and experienced the most severe beating with whips; they were in chains and imprisoned. [37]Some of these faith champions were brutally killed by stoning, being sawn in two or slaughtered by the sword. These lived in faith as they went about wearing goatskins and sheepskins for clothing. They lost everything they possessed, they endured great afflictions, and they were cruelly mistreated. [38]They wandered the earth living in the desert wilderness, in caves, on barren mountains and in holes in the earth. Truly, the world was not even worthy of them, not realizing who they were.

[39]These were the true heroes, commended for their faith, yet they lived in hope without receiving the fullness of what was promised them. [40]But now God has invited us to live in something better than what they had—faith's fullness! This is so that they could be brought to finished perfection alongside of us.

---

a Or "tortured with clubs (beaten to death)."

Twelve

The Great Cloud of Witnesses

¹As for us, we have all of these great witnesses[a] who encircle us like clouds, each affirming faith's reality.[b] So we must let go of every wound that has pierced us[c] and the sin we so easily fall into.[d] Then we will be able to run life's marathon race[e] with passion and determination, for the path has been already marked out before us.[f]

²We look away from the natural realm and we fasten our gaze onto Jesus who birthed faith within us and who leads us forward into faith's perfection.[g] His example is this: Because his heart was focused on the joy of knowing that you would be his,[h] he endured the agony of the cross and conquered its humiliation,[i] and now sits exalted at the right hand of the throne of God!

---

a 12:1 Or "martyrs."

b 12:1 Implied in the context.

c 12:1 Or "get rid of every arrow tip in us." The implication is carrying an arrow tip inside, a wound that weighs us down and keeps us from running our race with freedom.

d 12:1 Or "the sin that so cleverly entangles us." The Aramaic is "the sin that is ready (and waiting) for us." If this is speaking of one sin, the context would point to the sin of unbelief and doubting God's promises.

e 12:1 Or "obstacle course." The Greek word *agona* means agony or conflict. The assumption is this *race* will not be easy, but the proper path to run has been set before us.

f 12:1 The Aramaic is "the race (personally) appointed to us." God has a destiny for each of us that we are to give ourselves fully to reach.

g 12:2 Or "He is the Pioneer and Perfecter of faith."

h 12:2 Implied in the text. This was the joy of our salvation. He placed before his eyes the bliss we would forever share together with him, which empowered him to go through his agony.

i 12:2 As translated from the Aramaic. The Greek is "thinking nothing of its shame."

³So consider carefully how Jesus faced such intense opposition from sinners who opposed their own souls,ᵃ so that you won't become worn down and cave in under life's pressures, forgetting your destiny.ᵇ ⁴After all, you have not yet reached the point of sweating bloodᶜ in your opposition to sin. ⁵And have you forgotten his encouraging words spoken to you as his children? He said,

> **"My child, don't underestimate the value**
> > **of the discipline and training of the Lord God,**
> > **or get depressed when he has to correct you.ᵈ**
> **⁶For the Lord's training of your life**
> > **is the evidence of his faithful love.ᵉ**
> **And when he draws you to himself,**
> > **it proves you are his delightful child."ᶠ**

⁷Fully embrace God's correction as part of your training,ᵍ for he is doing what any loving father does for his children. For who has ever heard of a child who never had to be corrected?ʰ ⁸We all should welcome God's discipline as the validation of authentic sonship. For if we have never once endured his correction it only proves we are strangersⁱ and not sons.

⁹And isn't it true that we respect our earthly fathers even though they

---

a 12:3 Or "those who were their own stumbling block." As translated from the Aramaic.

b 12:3 Implied in the context.

c 12:4 Or "resisting until blood."

d 12:5 Or "when he puts you under scrutiny." The Aramaic is "Don't let your soul tremble (with dread) when your loyalty strays from him."

e 12:6 The Aramaic word used here means nurturing love, a mother's love. This passage shows both the strength of a father's love in how God disciplines us and the nurturing care of a mother's love. The Aramaic could be translated, "The Lord shows his nurturing love (mercy) to those he is sanctifying."

f 12:6 The Aramaic word for "draws you to himself is nagad, which can mean "scourge (severely punish)" or "to attract, to draw, or tug the heart." The Greek is "The Lord scourges (chastises) every son he receives." See also Proverbs 3:11–12.

g 12:7 Or "What you endure is meant to educate you."

h 12:7 The Aramaic can be translated "Who has ever heard of a child not approved by a father?"

i 12:8 As translated from the Aramaic. The Greek is "illegitimate."

corrected and disciplined us? Then we should demonstrate an even greater respect for God, our spiritual Father, as we submit to his life-giving disci-pline.[a] [10]Our parents corrected us for the short time of our childhood as it seemed good to them. But God corrects us throughout our lives for our own good, giving us an invitation to share his holiness. [11]Now all discipline[b] seems to be more pain than pleasure at the time, yet later it will produce a transformation of character, bringing a harvest of righteousness and peace[c] to those who yield to it.[d]

[12]So be made strong even in your weakness by lifting up your tired hands in prayer and worship.[e] And strengthen your weak knees,[f] [13]for as you keep walking forward on God's paths[g] all your stumbling ways will be divinely healed!

[14]In every relationship be swift to choose peace over competition,[h] and run swiftly toward holiness, for those who are not holy will not see the Lord.[i] [15]Watch over each other to make sure that no one misses the revelation of God's grace. And make sure no one lives with a root of bitterness[j] sprouting within them which will only cause trouble and poison the hearts of many.

[16]Be careful that no one among you lives in immorality, becoming careless about God's blessings, like Esau who traded away his rights as the firstborn for a simple meal. [17]And we know that later on when he wanted to inherit his father's blessing, he was turned away, even though he begged for it with bitter tears, for it was too late then to repent.[k]

---

a 12:9 See Proverbs 6:23.
b 12:10 Throughout this passage the word discipline can also be translated correction, instruction, and training.
c 12:11 See James 3:18.
d 12:11 Or "those who have endured its (gymnastic) training."
e 12:12 Implied in the text.
f 12:12 The Greek word used here can also mean "paralyzed knees."
g 12:13 See Isaiah 35:3; Proverbs 4:26.
h 12:14 See Psalm 34:14.
i 12:14 The Aramaic can be translated "no man will see into the Lord."
j 12:15 Or "resentment."
k 12:17 The Aramaic is "he found no place of restoration."

Entering into God's Presence

[18]As we approach God we leave the natural realm behind.[a] For we are not coming, as Moses did,[b] to a physical mountain with its burning fire, thick clouds of darkness and gloom, and with a raging whirlwind.[c] [19]We are not those who are being warned by the jarring blast of a trumpet and the thundering voice[d] warning the people to keep their distance;[e] the fearful voice that they begged to be silenced. [20]They couldn't handle God's command that said,

> **"If so much as an animal approaches the mountain**
> **it is to be stoned to death!"**

[21]The astounding phenomena Moses witnessed caused him to shudder with fear and he could only say, "I am trembling in terror!"[f]

[22]By contrast, we have already come[g] near to God in a totally different realm, the Zion-realm,[h] for we have entered the city of the Living God, which is the New Jerusalem in heaven![i] We have joined the festal

---

a 12:18 Implied in the context and supplied for the sake of English narrative.

b 12:18 Implied in the context and supplied for the sake of English narrative.

c 12:18 See Exodus 19; Amos 5:20; Deuteronomy 4:11 (LXX).

d 12:19 Or "the sound of words."

e 12:19 Implied in the context.

f 12:21 See Deuteronomy 9:19.

g 12:22 The Greek verb is in the perfect tense indicating that the fullness of our salvation and our entrance into God's heavenly realm has already taken place. See also Ephesians 2:6; Romans 8:29; Colossians 3:1–4.

h 12:22 Or "Mount Zion," which is not a literal mountain but an obvious metaphor for the realm of God's manifest presence. Mount Zion was once a Jebusite stronghold conquered by David (2 Samuel 5:6–9) who made it the capital for his kingdom. This is inside the walls of present day Jerusalem. Zion is used in both the Old and New Testaments as more than a location. Zion is referred to as the place of God's dwelling (Psalm 9:11; 48:1–2; 74:2; Isaiah 8:18). God's people are called "the daughters of Zion" (Song of Songs 3:11; Zechariah 9:9; John 12:15). Zion is the heavenly realm where God is manifest (Psalm 84:7; 102:16; 110:1–2; Revelation 14:1).

i 12:22 This is the fulfillment of Abraham's vision (Hebrews 11:10) and what Israel's ancestors had seen from afar (Hebrews 11:13). The New Jerusalem is not only a place, but a people who dwell with God in their midst. It is a city that is a bride or a bridal-city coming out of heaven to the earth (Revelation 21:9–14). We are not going to the New Jerusalem; we are going to be the New Jerusalem! The breastplate worn by the high priest over his heart with its precious stones was a miniature scale model of the New Jerusalem. The New Jerusalem is the amplification of that breastplate, a metaphor gathering of myriads of angels[a] in their joyous celebration![b]

²³And as members of the Church[c] of the Firstborn[d] all our names have been legally registered[e] as citizens of heaven! And we have come before God who judges all, and who lives among the spirits of the righteous who have been made perfect in his eyes![f]

²⁴And we have come to Jesus who established a new covenant with his blood sprinkled upon the mercy seat; blood that continues to speak from heaven, "Forgiveness," a better message than Abel's blood that cries from the earth, "Justice."[g]

²⁵Make very sure that you never refuse to listen to God when he speaks![h] For the God who spoke on earth from Sinai is the same God who now speaks from heaven. Those who heard him[i] speak his living Word on earth found nowhere to hide, so what chance is there for us to escape if we turn our backs on God and refuse to hear his warnings as he speaks from heaven?

²⁶The earth was rocked at the sound of his voice from the mountain, but now he has promised,

of transformed sons with their names engraved upon the precious stones. See Revelation 21:2–4. The Aramaic reads, "You have already received communion on Mount Zion."

a 12:22 See Deuteronomy 33:2; Daniel 7:10; Jude 14;and Revelation 5:11.

b 12:22 This is much more than an assembly of angels. The Greek word *panēgyris* was used in classic Greek literature for civic festivals and celebrations which drew people from all parts of the empire and included all the various social classes. These were times of great joy and festivities with people wearing white robes and with garlands on their heads. (See *Philo; Gaius* 12; *Isocrates; Panegyricus* 43, 46.) This verse teaches that we have already entered into the festival of angelic bliss through Jesus Christ.

c 12:23 This is the Greek word *ekklēsia,* which is commonly used for church. However, *ekklēsia* means more than a church meeting, for it signified in Greek culture the governing assembly which had the authority to make decisions for the entire city. See Matthew 16:18.

d 12:23 This is Jesus who is God's uniquely Firstborn (Hebrews 1:6). In Christ we are all the firstborn and have all the rights and blessings that Jesus has.

e 12:23 Or "whose names are written in heaven." There are many books in heaven. See Exodus 32:32; Psalm 69:28; 87:6; Daniel 12:1; Luke 10:20; Philippians 4:3; Revelation 3:5; 13:8; 17:8; 20:12,15; 21:27.

f 12:23 The Aramaic is "and to the Spirit who has perfected the righteous ones."

g 12:24 See Genesis 4:10.

h 12:25 Or "don't turn your back on the Speaker."

i 12:25 The Greek is somewhat ambiguous with the possibility that it is Moses or even Christ who is speaking. The context seems to imply however that it is God himself who speaks both from Sinai and from heaven.

> "Once and for all I will not only shake
>   the systems of the world,[a]
>   but also the unseen powers in the heavenly realm!"[b]

[27]Now this phrase "once and for all" clearly indicates the final removal of things that are shaking, that is, the old order,[c] so only what is unshakeable will remain. [28]Since we are receiving our rights[d] to an unshakeable kingdom[e] we should be extremely thankful and offer God the purest worship that delights his heart[f] as we lay down our lives in absolute surrender, filled with awe.[g] [29]For our God is a holy, devouring Fire![h]

---

a 12:26 Or "earth." Although earthquakes are prophesied to come (Matthew 24:7; Mark 13:8; Luke 21:11; Revelation 8:5; 11:13, 19; 16:18) the prophet is most likely using a metaphoric term for the world's systems (finance, military, governments, religious, etc.). The message of the gospel has shaken the world's foundations as it includes an unshakeable kingdom rising on the earth. Kings of the earth have placed their crowns down before the cross of a Man who was crucified as a common criminal. The power of the gospel is still shaking the world.

b 12:26 Implied in the text. It is not God's power or throne being shaken, but invisible forces of darkness in the heavenly realm. See Haggai 2:6; Ephesians 6:12.

c 12:27 Or "things that have been made."

d 12:28 The Greek word *paralambano* is often used in classical Greek literature for heirs who have the "rights of succession (to a throne)." (See Arist. Pol. 3.14.12; Hdt. 2.120)

e 12:28 See Daniel 7:18.

f 12:28 Or "offer pleasing service to God."

g 12:28 The Aramaic is "We have received grace to serve and we please God in awe and tender devotion (submission)."

h 12:29 The Aramaic is "consuming Light." See also Deuteronomy 4:24; 9:3.

Thirteen

Live Pleasing to God

[1]No matter what, make room in your heart to love every believer. [2]And show hospitality to strangers, for they may be angels from God showing up as your guests.[a] [3]Identify with those who are in prison as though you were there suffering with them, and those who are mistreated as if you could feel their pain.[b]

[4]Honor the sanctity of marriage and keep your vows of purity to one another, for God will judge sexual immorality in any form, whether single or married.

[5]Don't be obsessed with money but live content with what you have, for you always have God's presence. For hasn't he promised you,

> **"I will never leave you alone, never! And I will not loosen my grip on your life!"[c]**

[6]So we can say with great confidence:

> **"I know the Lord is for me**
> **and I will never be afraid**
> **of what people may do to me!"[d]**

---

a 13:2 The Aramaic is "for this is how you are worthy to receive angels while awake." See also Matthew 25:35.

b 13:3 The Aramaic is "as if you were people who wear their bodies (vulnerable to their pain)."

c 13:5 Or "hand" as translated from the Aramaic. See also Deuteronomy 31:6, 8.

d 13:6 See Psalm 118:6–7.

[7]Don't forget the example of your spiritual leaders who have spoken God's messages to you, take a close look at how their lives ended,[a] and then follow their walk of faith.

[8]Jesus, the Anointed One, is always the same—yesterday, today, and forever.[b] [9]So don't let anyone lead you astray with all sorts of novel and exotic teachings. It is more beautiful to feast on grace and be inwardly strengthened than to be obsessed with dietary rules[c] which in themselves have no lasting benefit.

[10]We feast on a sacrifice at our spiritual altar, but those who serve as priests in the old system of worship have no right to eat of it. [11]For the high priest carries the blood of animals into the holiest chamber as a sacrifice for sin, and then burns the bodies of the animals outside the city.[d] [12]And Jesus, our sin-sacrifice, also suffered death outside the city walls to make us holy by his own blood.

[13]So we must arise and join him outside the religious "walls" and bear his disgrace.[e] [14]For we have no city here on earth to be our permanent home, but we seek the city that is destined to come.[f] [15]So we no longer offer up a steady stream of blood sacrifices,[g] but through Jesus, we will offer up to God a steady stream of praise sacrifices—these are "the lambs"[h] we offer from our lips that celebrate his name![i]

[16]We will show mercy to the poor[j] and not miss an opportunity to do acts of kindness for others, for these are the true sacrifices that delight God's heart.

---

a 13:7 Or "consider the outcome (spiritual fruit) of the way they lived."
b 13:8 The Aramaic is "Jesus the Messiah is the fulfillment of yesterday, today, and forever."
c 13:9 Or "ceremonial foods."
d 13:11 See Leviticus 16:14, 27.
e 13:13 Or "carry his insults" or "endure the abuse he suffered."
f 13:14 Or "the city that is intended." The Aramaic is "the city which is anxiously awaited."
g 13:15 Implied in the context and supplied to clarify the contrast.
h 13:15 As translated from the Aramaic. The Greek is "the fruit of our lips."
i 13:15 See Psalm 50:14, 23.
j 13:16 As translated from the Aramaic.

¹⁷Obey your spiritual leaders and recognize their authority, for they keep watch over your soul without resting ᵃ since they will have to give an account to God for their work. So it will benefit you when you make their work a pleasure and not a heavy burden.

¹⁸And keep praying for us that we continue to live with a clear conscience, for we desire to live honorably in all that we do. ¹⁹And I especially ask you to pray that God would send me back to you very soon.

Apostolic Blessing and Conclusion

²⁰Now may the God who brought us peace by raising from the dead our Lord Jesus Christ so that he would be the Great Shepherd of his flock; and by the power of the blood of the eternal covenant ²¹may he work perfection into every part of you giving you all that you need to fulfill your destiny. And may he express through you all that is excellent and pleasing ᵇ to him through your life-union with Jesus the Anointed One who is to receive all glory forever! Amen!

²²My dear brothers and sisters, I urge you to let your spirits flow through this message of love ᶜ that I've written to you in these few words. ²³I want you to know that our brother Timothy is free again and as soon as he arrives here we'll come together to see you. We extend our greetings to all your leaders and all the holy believers. ²⁴The Italian believers also send their greetings. ᵈ Now may God's wonderful grace be poured out upon you all! Amen!

---

a 13:17 The Greek word *agrypnein* is often used for staying awake through the night.
b 13:21 The Aramaic is "beautiful."
c 13:22 As translated from the Aramaic.
d 13:24 The Aramaic has this sentence at the end, "The end of the letter to the Hebrews written from Italy."

James
(Jacob)

Translator's Introduction to James (Jacob)

AT A GLANCE

Author: James, brother of Jesus

Audience: Jewish Christians

Date: AD 45–47

Type of Literature: A wisdom letter

Major Themes: Wisdom, trials, the Law, faith and works, poverty and wealth

Outline:

Greeting — 1:1
Introducing the Three Themes: Wealth, Wisdom, Trials — 1:2–27
Theme 1: Riches and Poverty — 2:1–26
Theme 2: Wisdom and Speech — 3:1–4:12
Theme 3: Trials and Temptation — 4:13–5:18
Closing — 5:19–20

ABOUT JAMES (JACOB)

The Holy Spirit speaks through the Bible, God's Holy Word. His life-giving expression comes through each verse, and we are changed by receiving the Word of God. The book of James is rich with life-changing revelation, a feast to strengthen you and keep you on course. We thank God that the book of James is included in our Bibles for it gives us the understanding of the power of faith to produce good works. Faith works!

Actually, this letter is titled, Jacob. By calling this book James instead of Jacob the church loses a vital component of our Jewish beginnings. There is no "James" in Greek; it is Jacob. We would never say that God is the God of Abraham, Isaac, and James. Neither should we call this letter James, when it is in fact, the letter of Jacob!

Most scholars don't believe that he was a believer until after Jesus died and rose again (see John 7:5). Can you imagine growing up with the Son of God and not knowing it? Yet today many are able to see the works of Jesus all around them and still remain unconvinced. However, James (Jacob) did become a powerful voice in the early church as the presiding apostle of the church of Jerusalem. And like his Older Brother, he also was killed for his faith, according to the Jewish historian Josephus in AD 62.

The book of James (Jacob) and the book of Galatians are considered to be the first letters penned by the apostles most likely sometime between AD 45–47. So when we read this letter we are reading the earliest insights of the first generation of followers of Jesus who were mostly Jews.

James (Jacob) gives us practical truths about what it means to be declared righteous by God. He gives us many clear insights on faith and walking in the truth. You might want to view the this book as the New Testament version of Proverbs, for much of his writings speak of God's heavenly wisdom that can transform us.

I have fallen in love with Jesus! And I love his brother Jacob. I think you will too.

PURPOSE

Although the book of James is a letter, it reads more like a wisdom sermon addressing a number of crucial topics relevant to Jewish Christians using familiar language from the Old Testament. His letter was similar to so-called *diaspora letters* from ancient times written to the scattered Jewish people. Like those, it offers comfort and hope during persecution and trials; encourages faithful obedience to God; and provides spiritual instruction and encouragement on important matters relating to the unity and life of the church.

AUTHOR AND AUDIENCE

Although debated by some, it is believed that the James (Jacob) who wrote this book (also known as James the Just) was the half-brother of our Lord Jesus referred to in Galatians 1:19 and in Mark 6:3. This is amazing to think that the actual half-brother of our Lord and Savior gives us truth to live by. We should listen to what James (Jacob) has to say and take it to heart!

Given the dominant Jewish flavor of the letter, it appears he originally targeted Jewish Christians. James said, "I'm writing to all the twelve tribes of Israel who have been sown as seeds among the nations." His thoughts were meant to reach out to all the Christians who converted from Judaism who were scattered throughout the Roman empire, calling their attention to the fulfillment of the promises for a Messiah in Jesus.

MAJOR THEMES

Wisdom from Above: The Greek word for wisdom, *sophia*, occurs four times in James' letter. His letter could be considered a wisdom sermon, for the style of the letter is similar to the Proverbs. Throughout his letter James taps into the long tradition of Jewish wisdom and applies it to various practical topics for wise Christian living. He recognizes wisdom is necessary for trying circumstances; it involves insight into God's purposes and leads to spiritual maturity; and God is the source of all true wisdom.

Testing and Trials: In many ways, the wisdom-letter of James is written to help guide those whose faith in God is being threatened by daily struggles and hardship. The kinds of testing and trials James speaks of can range from religious persecution to financial difficulties, from health problems to even spiritual oppression. James is clear such experiences are never a waste, there's a goal: Spiritual maturity born through perseverance.

The Law of Moses: While James doesn't directly refer to the law of the Old Testament, he does refer to "the royal law of love as given to us in this Scripture: 'You must love and value your neighbor'" (2:8). Of course Jesus Christ himself gave us this royal law, which he said summed up all the Law and Prophets. And for James, anything that violates this law is as serious as violating any of the Ten Commandments. The law is relevant to Christian living not as legalistic rules and rituals, but as love of neighbor and God.

Faith and Good Deeds: One of the ongoing debates with James' letter is whether it contradicts the teachings of Paul and his theology of salvation by faith alone. While some of what James says may seem like a contradiction, it isn't. Instead of undermining and opposing Paul's teaching that works cannot save, James explains the kind of faith that does. "Faith that doesn't involve actions is phony," James argues. Faith that saves is a faith that works!

Poverty and Wealth: One of the major concerns of James seemed to be the huge gap between the rich and poor, even within the church. He encourages poor believers that they have been blessed with every privilege from God, though society may dismiss them. And to the rich he reminds them no amount of wealth from below could buy what they've been given from above. James also writes against favoritism in the church of any kind, especially based on the size of one's pocketbook or the brand of their clothes.

Enjoy this wonderful book by the brother of our Lord.

—Dr. Brian Simmons

One

Faith and Wisdom

[1]Greetings! My name is Jacob,[a] and I'm a love-slave of God and of the Lord Jesus Christ. I'm writing to all the twelve tribes of Israel who have been sown as seeds[b] among the nations.

[2]My fellow believers, when it seems as though you are facing nothing but difficulties see it as an invaluable opportunity to experience the greatest joy that you can! [3]For you know that when your faith is tested[c] it stirs up power within you to endure all things. [4]And then as your endurance grows even stronger it will release perfection into every part of your being until there is nothing missing and nothing lacking.

[5]And if anyone longs to be wise, ask God for wisdom and he will give it! He won't see your lack of wisdom as an opportunity to scold you over your failures but he will overwhelm your failures with his generous grace.[d] [6]Just make sure you ask empowered by confident faith without doubting that you will receive. For the ambivalent person believes one minute and doubts the next. Being undecided makes you become like the rough seas driven and tossed by the wind. You're up one minute and tossed down the next. [7-8]When you are half-hearted and wavering it leaves you unstable.[e]

---

a 1:1 James is actually the Hebrew name Jacob, the name of the man who had twelve sons that formed the twelve tribes of Israel.

b 1:1 As translated from the Aramaic, which was the language spoken by Jesus and his disciples.

c 1:3 Or "when faith passes the test."

d 1:5 Or "with an open hand."

e 1:7–8 Or "restless" or "disengaged."

Can you really expect to receive anything from the Lord when you're in that condition?

⁹The believer who is poor still has reasons to boast, for he has been placed on high. ¹⁰But those who are rich should boast in how God has brought them low and humbled them, for all their earthly glory will one day fade away like a wildflower in the meadow. ¹¹For as the scorching heat of the sun causes the petals of the wildflower to fall off and lose its appearance of beauty,ª so the rich in the midst of their pursuit of wealth will wither away.

¹²If your faith remains strong, even while surrounded by life's difficulties, you will continue to experience the untold blessings of God! True happiness comes as you pass the test with faith, and receive the victorious crown of life promised to every lover of God!

¹³When you are tempted don't ever say, "God is tempting me," for God is incapable of being tempted by evil and he is never the source of temptation. ¹⁴Instead it is each person's own desires and thoughts that drag them into evil and lureᵇ them away into darkness. ¹⁵Evil desires give birth to evil actions. And when sin is fully mature it can murder you! ¹⁶So my friends, don't be fooled by your own desires!

¹⁷Every giftᶜ God freely gives us is good and perfect,ᵈ streaming down from the Father of Lights,ᵉ who shines from the heavens with no hidden

---

a 1:11 In the land of the Bible there were many deserts with arid land. The rainy season is quite short and the burning heat of the sun scorched the earth until the next season of rain arrived. We live in a constantly changing world with riches and beauty quickly fading. Our hope is set on things above.

b 1:14 Or "hooked by the bait of evil from their own desires."

c 1:17 Or "legacy."

d 1:17 The Aramaic word used here, mshamlaita, means "complete, perfect, wholesome, abundant, sufficient, enough, and perfect."

e 1:17 Jesus calls us the light of the world (Matthew 5:14–16) and Paul describes believers as "shining lights" in this world. God is our Father, he created angels but he brought us into new birth. The Greek word "anōthen (from above)" is used by Jesus in describing to Nicodemus that we are born from above. We are lights born from above. See also John 3:7.

shadow or darkness[a] and is never subject to change. [18]God was delighted[b] to give us birth by the truth of his infallible Word[c] so that we would fulfill his chosen destiny for us and become the favorite ones out of all his creation![d]

[19]My dearest brothers and sisters, take this to heart: Be quick to listen,[e] but slow to speak. And be slow to become angry, [20]for human anger is never a legitimate tool to promote God's righteous purpose.[f] [21]So this is why we abandon everything morally impure[g] and all forms of wicked conduct.[h] Instead, with a sensitive spirit[i] we absorb God's Manifestation, which has been implanted within our nature, for the Word of Life has power to continually deliver us.[j]

[22]Don't just listen to the Word of Truth and not respond to it, for that is the essence of self-deception. So always let his Word become like poetry written and fulfilled by your life![k]

[23]If you listen to the Word and don't live out the message you hear, you become like the person who looks in the mirror of the Word to discover the reflection of his face in the beginning.[l] [24]*You perceive how God sees you in*

---

a 1:17 Or "shadow of turning." The implication is there is nothing that you will find wrong with God, nothing in him that could even remotely appear to be evil hiding. The more you get to know him the more you realize how beautiful and holy he is.

b 1:18 Or "God having decided gave us birth." The comparison in this passage is striking. Sin gives birth to death, God from his pure desires gives us birth to bring him glory.

c 1:18 The Aramaic can be translated "the Word of the rainbow-sign." That is, the unbreakable new covenant promises we have as new creatures in Christ.

d 1:18 Or "a kind of firstfruits of his creations" or "the pledge (down-payment) of a still further creation (a more complete harvest)."

e 1:19 Although the Greek does not supply an object we are to *listen* to, it is obvious in the context that we should *listen* to one another, to God's voice, and to his Word. May God give us listening hearts.

f 1:20 Or "God's righteousness will never attach itself to human anger."

g 1:21 The Aramaic word used here can mean "demonic activities."

h 1:21 Or "excesses of evil."

i 1:21 Due to the Greek sentence construction, this clause may refer to what preceded it, "abandon... all forms of wicked conduct with a gentle (meek) heart."

j 1:21 Or "save our souls." The Greek uses the effective aorist active infinitive σωσαι [sōsai] from σωζω [sōzō]) and could refer to the ultimate salvation of our souls (personality, emotions, thoughts) and/or our eternal salvation.

k 1:22 Or "be a poet (doer) of the Word."

l 1:23 Or "realizing his beginning (genesis) face" or "studying the face he was born with."

the mirror of the Word,[a] but then you go out and forget[b] your divine origin. [25]But those who set their gaze deeply into the perfecting law of liberty,[c] are fascinated by and respond to the truth they hear and are strengthened by it—they experience God's blessing in all that they do![d]

[26]If someone believes they have a relationship with God but fails to guard his words then his heart is drifting away and his religion is shallow and empty.[e]

[27]True spirituality[f] that is pure in the eyes of our Father-God is to make a difference in the lives of the orphans,[g] and widows in their troubles, and to refuse to be corrupted by the world's values.

---

a 1:24 Implied in the text. For the believer, seeing the "man in the mirror" is seeing how God sees us from the beginning, even before the fall of Adam which resulted in sin's devastation to human hearts. The man in the mirror is the new creation man.

b 1:24 The Aramaic is "drift away from."

c 1:25 This is referred to as the "royal law of love" in 2:8 and the "law of freedom" in 2:12.

d 1:25 See Luke 11:28.

e 1:26 As translated from the Aramaic. The Greek is "If one presumes to be religious but doesn't guard his tongue, he deceives himself and his religion is useless."

f 1:27 The Aramaic is "True ministry."

g 1:27 The Greek word *orhpanos* means "the fatherless" or "the comfortless."

Two

___

The Royal Law of Love Excludes Prejudice

¹My dear brothers and sisters, fellow believers in our glorious Lord Jesus Christ—how could we say that we have faith in him and yet we favor one group of people above another?[a] ²Suppose an influential man comes into your worship meeting wearing gold rings and expensive clothing, and also a homeless man in shabby clothes comes in. ³If you show special attention to the rich man in expensive clothes and say, "Here's a seat of honor for you right up front!" but you turn and say to the poor beggar dressed in rags, "You can stand over here," or "Sit over there on the floor in the back,"[b] ⁴then you've demonstrated gross prejudice among yourselves and used evil standards of judgment!

⁵So listen carefully, my dear brothers and sisters, hasn't God chosen[c] the poor in the world's eyes to be those who are rich in faith?[d] And won't they be the heirs of the kingdom-realm he promised to those who love him? ⁶But yet you insult and shun the poor in your efforts to impress the rich![e] Isn't it the wealthy who exploit you and drag you into court? ⁷Aren't they the very ones who blaspheme the beautiful name of the One you now belong to?[f]

___

a 2:1 The Aramaic is "Don't be taken in by the face-mask of people, but hold to the faith in the glory of our Lord Jesus the Messiah."

b 2:3 The Aramaic is "Sit on the floor before our footstool."

c 2:5 The Greek word for "chosen" is *eklegomai*, which is a form of *lego* (speak).

d 2:5 See 1 Corinthians 1:27–28.

e 2:6 Implied in the context. See also 1 Corinthians 11:22.

f 2:7 Or "the worthy name which was invoked over you (at your baptism)."

⁸Your calling is to fulfill the royal law of love[a] as given to us in this Scripture:

"You must love and value your neighbor as you love and value yourself!"[b]

For keeping this law is the noble way to live. ⁹But when you show prejudice you commit sin and you violate this royal law of love!

¹⁰For the one who attempts to keep all of the law of Moses but fails in just one point has become guilty of breaking the law in every respect! ¹¹For the same One who tells us, **"Do not commit adultery,"** also said, **"Do not murder."**[c] Now if you don't commit adultery but do commit murder, you are still guilty as a law-breaker. ¹²So we must both speak and act in every respect like those who are destined to be tried by the perfect law of liberty, ¹³and remember that judgment is merciless for the one who judges others without mercy. So by showing mercy you take dominion over judgment![d]

Faith Works

¹⁴My dear brothers and sisters, what good is it if someone claims to have faith but demonstrates no good works to prove it? How could this kind of faith save anyone? ¹⁵For example, if a brother or sister in the faith is poorly clothed and hungry ¹⁶and you leave them saying, "Good-bye. I hope you stay warm and have plenty to eat," but you don't provide them with a coat or even a cup of soup, what good is your faith? ¹⁷So then faith that doesn't involve actions is phony.[e]

¹⁸But someone might object and say, "One person has faith and

---

a 2:8 It is a royal law because it is given by our King, but since he has made us kings and priests, it becomes the royal law of love given to his royal sons and daughters who are heirs with him.

b 2:8 See Leviticus 19:18; Matthew 19:19; 22:39; Mark 12:31; Luke 10:27; Romans 13:9; Galatians 5:14.

c 2:11 See Exodus 20:13–14.

d 2:13 As translated from the Aramaic. The Greek is "Mercy triumphs over judgment."

e 2:17 Or "dead (fruitless)." See also v. 20.

another person has works."[a] Go ahead then and prove to me that you have faith without works and I will show you faith by my works as proof that I believe. [19]You can believe all you want that there is one true God,[b] that's wonderful! But even the demons know this and tremble with fear before him,[c] yet they're unchanged—they remain demons.[d]

[20]O feeble sons of Adam,[e] do you need further evidence that faith divorced from good works is phony? [21]Wasn't our ancestor Abraham found righteous before God because of his works when he offered his son Isaac on the altar? [22]Can't you see how his actions cooperated with his faith and by his actions faith found its full expression? [23]So in this way the Scripture was fulfilled:

Because Abraham believed God, his faith was exchanged for God's righteousness.[f]

So he became known as the lover of God![g] [24]So now it's clear that a person is seen as righteous in God's eyes not merely by faith alone, but by his works.

[25]And the same is true of the prostitute named Rahab who was found righteous in God's eyes by her works, for she received the spies into her home and helped them escape from the city by another route.[h] [26]For just as a human body without the spirit is a dead corpse, so faith without the expression of good works is dead!

---

a 2:18 Many scholars conclude that the ambiguity of the Greek text makes this the most difficult verse in all of James and perhaps in all of the New Testament to translate.

b 2:19 Or "that God is one," which is the Jewish *Shema*□ (see Deuteronomy 6:4).

c 2:19 The Aramaic is "they writhe on their bellies in the dirt!"

d 2:19 Implied in the context.

e 2:20 As translated from the Aramaic. The Greek is "O empty man."

f 2:23 Or "Abraham's faith was credited to his account for righteousness." See Genesis 15:6

g 2:23 As translated from the Aramaic. Although the Greek text is most often translated "friend of God," the Greek word *philos* can also be used as the love that bonds friends together. See also 2 Chronicles 20:7; Isaiah 41:18; Daniel 3:35 (LXX).

h 2:25 See Joshua 2.

Three

The Power of Your Words

¹My dear brothers and sisters, don't be so eager to become a teacher in the church since you know that we who teach are held to a higher standard of judgment. ²We all fail in many areas, but especially with our words. Yet if we're able to bridle the words we say we are powerful enough to control ourselves in every way, and that means our character is mature and fully developed. ³Horses have bits and bridles in their mouths so that we can control and guide their large body. ⁴And the same with mighty ships, though they are massive and driven by fierce winds, yet they are steered by a tiny rudder at the direction of the person at the helm.

⁵And so the tongue is a small part of the body yet it carries great power![a] Just think of how a small flame can set a huge forest ablaze. ⁶And the tongue is a fire! It can be compared to the sum total of wickedness[b] and is the most dangerous part of our human body. It corrupts the entire body[c] and is a hellish flame![d] It releases a fire that can burn throughout the course of human existence.[e]

---

a 3:5 Or "boasts of great things." The Aramaic is "the tongue has dominion."
b 3:6 As translated from the Latin Vulgate. The Greek is "a world of wrongdoing."
c 3:6 It is possible that the body James refers to here is the body of believers (a local church).
d 3:6 Or "is set ablaze by Gehenna (hell)." The Aramaic does not mention *Gehenna* but is simply "burns with fire." Gehenna is taken from the concept of "The Valley of Hinnom" where rubbish was burned outside the city of Jerusalem, becoming a Hebrew metaphor for the fires of hell.
e 3:6 The Aramaic is "a fire that passes through successive generations, rolling on like wheels."

[7]For every wild animal on earth including birds, creeping reptiles, and creatures of the sea and land[a] have all been overpowered and tamed by humans, [8]but the tongue is not able to be tamed. It's a fickle, unrestrained evil that spews out words full of toxic poison! [9]We use our tongue to praise God our Father[b] and then turn around and curse a person who was made in his very image![c] [10]Out of the same mouth we pour out words of praise one minute and curses the next. My brothers and sister, this should never be!

[11–12]Would you look for olives hanging on a fig tree or go to pick figs from a grapevine? Is it possible that fresh and bitter water can flow out of the same spring? So neither can a bitter spring produce fresh water.[d]

Wisdom from Above

[13]If you consider yourself to be wise and one who understands the ways of God, advertise it with a beautiful, fruitful[e] life guided by wisdom's gentleness. Never brag or boast about what you've done and you'll prove that you're truly wise. [14]But if there is bitter jealousy or competition hiding in your heart, then don't deny it and try to compensate for it by boasting and being phony. [15]For that has nothing to do with God's heavenly wisdom but can best be described as the wisdom of this world, both selfish[f] and devilish.[g] [16]So wherever jealousy[h] and selfishness are uncovered, you will also find many troubles[i] and every kind of meanness.

---

a 3:7 Implied in the Greek and made explicit in the Aramaic.
b 3:9 Some Greek manuscripts have "Lord and Father." The Aramaic is "Lord God (MarYah, the Aramaic equivalent to Yahweh).
c 3:9 The Aramaic can be translated "we curse a person and pretend to be God!"
d 3:11–12 As translated from the Aramaic.
e 3:13 As translated from the Aramaic.
f 3:15 Or "unspiritual."
g 3:15 Or "behaves like a demon."
h 3:16 The Greek word for jealousy implies an obsession to promote one's self at the expense of others.
i 3:16 The Aramaic is "chaos." The Greek can be translated "instability" or "disorder."

¹⁷But the wisdom from above is always pure,ᵃ filled with peace, considerate and teachable.ᵇ It is filled with loveᶜ and never displays prejudice or hypocrisyᵈ in any form ¹⁸and it always bears the beautiful harvest of righteousness! Good seeds of wisdom's fruit will be planted with peaceful acts by those who cherish making peace.

---

a 3:17 Or "holy."
b 3:17 A beautiful concept that means "easy to correct" or "ready to be convinced" or "willing to yield to others." Is this true of your life?
c 3:17 As translated from the Aramaic. The Greek is "mercy."
d 3:17 Or "never wears a mask."

Four

———

Living Close to God

¹What is the cause of your conflicts and quarrels with each other? Doesn't the battle begin inside of you as you fight to have your own way and fulfill your own desires? ²You jealously want what others have so you begin to see yourself as better than others. You scheme with envy and harm[a] others to selfishly obtain what you crave—that's why you quarrel and fight. And all the time you don't obtain what you want because you won't ask God for it! ³And if you ask, you won't receive it for you're asking with corrupt motives, seeking only to fulfill your own selfish desires. ⁴You have become spiritual adulterers who are having an affair, an unholy relationship with the world. Don't you know that flirting with the world's values places you at odds with God? Whoever chooses to be the world's friend makes himself God's enemy!

⁵Does the Scripture mean nothing to you that says, **"The Spirit that God breathed into our hearts is a jealous Lover who intensely desires to have more and more of us"?**[b]

---

a 4:2 Or "kill," however, the Greek word for *kill* and *envy* are almost the same.

b 4:5 Although it is difficult to find a verse from the Old Testament that reads exactly how James quotes it, the possibility remains that it becomes a general statement of what the Bible teaches, or even a quotation from an older translation not available today.

⁶But he continues to pour out more and more grace*ᵃ* upon us. For it says,

**God resists you when you are proud
but continually pours out grace when you are humble."***ᵇ*

⁷So then, surrender to God. Stand up to the Devil and resist him and he will turn and run away from you. ⁸Move your heart closer and closer to God, and he will come even closer to you.*ᶜ* But make sure you cleanse your life, you sinners, and keep your heart pure and stop doubting.*ᵈ* ⁹Feel the pain of your sin, be sorrowful and weep! Let your joking around*ᵉ* be turned into mourning and your joy into deep humiliation. ¹⁰Be willing to be made low before the Lord and he will exalt you!

¹¹Dear friends, as part of God's family, never speak against another family member, for when you slander a brother or sister you violate*ᶠ* God's law of love.*ᵍ* And your duty is not to make yourself a judge of the law of love*ʰ* by saying that it doesn't apply to you,*ⁱ* *but your duty is to obey it!ʲ* ¹²There is only one true Lawgiver and Judge, the One who has the power to save and destroy—so who do you think you are to judge your neighbor?

¹³Listen, those of you who are boasting, "Today or tomorrow we'll go to another city and spend some time and go into business and make heaps of profit!" ¹⁴But you don't have a clue what tomorrow may bring. For your fleeting life is but a warm breath of air that is visible in the cold only for a

---

a 4:6 Or "he gives us a greater gift" or "the grace (favor) he gives us is stronger."
b 4:6 See Proverbs 3:34.
c 4:8 The Aramaic is "and he will be touching you."
d 4:8 Or "you double-minded."
e 4:9 As translated from the Aramaic.
f 4:11 Or "speak against."
g 4:11 Implied in the context.
h 4:11 Implied in the context. See also Leviticus 19:18; James 4:8.
i 4:11 Or "to be a judge of the law."
j 4:11 Implied in the argument James makes to refrain from being a judge of the law.

moment and then vanishes! [15]Instead you should say, "Our tomorrows are in the Lord's hands and if he is willing we will live life to its fullest and do this or that." [16]But here you are, boasting in your ignorance, for to be presumptuous about what you'll do tomorrow is evil!

[17]So if you know of an opportunity to do the right thing today, yet you refrain from doing it, you're guilty of sin.

Five
___

Warning to the Rich

[1]Listen all you who are rich, for it's time to weep and howl over the misery[a] that will overtake you! [2]Your riches lie rotting, your fine clothing eaten by moths, [3]and your gold and silver are corroded as a witness against you. You have hoarded up treasure for the last days but it will become a fire to burn your flesh. [4]Listen! Can't you hear the cries of the laborers[b] over the wages you fraudulently held back from those who worked for you?[c] The cries for justice of those you've cheated have reached the ears of the Lord of Armies![d]

[5]You have indulged yourselves with every luxury and pleasure this world offers, but you're only stuffing your heart full for a day of slaughter. [6]You have condemned and murdered good and innocent people[e] who had no power to defend themselves.[f]

---

a 5:1 The Aramaic word can refer to demonic torment.
b 5:4 Or "the reapers (of your fields)."
c 5:4 Or "those who worked in your fields."
d 5:4 Or "Lord Sabaoth."
e 5:6 Or "the righteous one," a possible reference to the death of Jesus.
f 5:6 Or "will not (God) resist you?"

⁷Meanwhile, brothers and sisters, we must be patient and filled with expectation as we wait for the appearing[a] of the Lord. Think about the farmer who has to patiently wait for the earth's harvest as it ripens because of the early and latter rains. ⁸So you also keep your hopes high and be patient, for the presence of the Lord is drawing closer.[b] ⁹Since each of you are part of God's family never complain or grumble about each other[c] so that judgment will not come on you, for the true Judge is near and very ready to appear![d]

¹⁰My brothers and sisters, take[e] the prophets as your mentors. They have prophesied in the name of the Lord[f] and it brought them great sufferings[g] yet they patiently endured. ¹¹We honor them as our heroes[h] because they remained faithful even while enduring great sufferings. And you have heard of all that Job went through and we can now see that the Lord ultimately treated him with wonderful kindness, revealing how tenderhearted he really is![i]

¹²Above all we must be those who never need to verify our speech as truthful by swearing by the heavens or the earth or any other oath.[j] But instead we must be so full of integrity[k] that our "Yes" or "No" is convincing enough and we do not stumble into hypocrisy.[l]

---

a 5:7 This is the abstract Greek word *parousia* which can mean "arrival, presence, becoming manifest, appearing." *Parousia* is taken from the present participle *pareina* a compound word of *para* (beside) and *einai* (to be seen, made visible). It has little to do with distance or space, but with becoming visible, such as an uncovering or revealing what is nearby. It is commonly used for the return of our Lord Jesus Christ.

b 5:8 Or "near at hand." The Greek word *engizo* is taken from the word *eggus*, which means to take by the hand, to throttle, or to hold the reins. See *Strong's Concordance* 1448 and 1451.

c 5:9 Or "don't blame others (for your troubles)."

d 5:9 Or "at the gate."

e 5:10 Or "receive."

f 5:10 That is, by the Lord's authority. See also verse 14.

g 5:10 Implied in the text.

h 5:11 Or "we regard them as blessed."

i 5:11 See Exodus 34:6; Psalm 86:15.

j 5:12 See Matthew 5:34.

k 5:12 Implied in the text.

l 5:12 Some Greek manuscripts read, "stumble into hypocrisy," while others have, "stumble into judgment."

Prayer for the Sick

[13]Are there any believers in your fellowship suffering great hardship and distress? Encourage them to pray![a] Are there happy, cheerful ones among you? Encourage them to sing out their praises![b] [14]Are there any sick among you? Then ask the elders of the church to come and pray over the sick and anoint them with oil in the name of our Lord. [15]And the prayer of faith[c] will heal the sick[d] and the Lord will raise them up,[e] and if they have committed sins[f] they will be forgiven.[g]

[16]Confess and acknowledge how you have offended one another[h] and then pray for one another to be instantly healed,[i] for tremendous power is released through the passionate, heartfelt prayer of a godly believer!

[17]Elijah was a man with human frailties, just like all of us, but he prayed and received supernatural answers.[j] He actually shut the heavens over the land so there would be no rain for three and a half years! [18]Then he prayed again and the skies opened up over the land so that the rain came again and produced the harvest.

[19]Finally, as members of God's beloved family, we must go after the one who wanders from the truth and bring him back. [20]For the one who

---

a 5:13 See Luke 18:1; 1 Corinthians 14:14–15.
b 5:13 Or "pluck the strings of a harp" or "sing a psalm."
c 5:15 Or "the claim of faith."
d 5:15 This is not the Greek usually used for sickness or disease. The word *kamno* can also mean "those who are weary and worn down," and in the context could possibly refer to believers who have been arguing with each other, leaving them spiritually weak.
e 5:15 That is, restore them to health. This could be a subtle hint of a resurrection.
f 5:15 Or "doer of sin." There is a clear implication in this passage that the sickness (weakness) referred to is the result of sin. See also 1 Corinthians 11:18–32.
g 5:15 This may be speaking of the church elders that are forgiving the arguing believers and restoring them back into fellowship.
h 5:16 As translated from the Aramaic, which uses a word that can be translated "faults" or "folly" or "offenses." The Critical Greek text is "confess your sins."
i 5:16 Or "restored."
j 5:17 Or "he prayed with prayer (intensity)."

restores the sinning believer back to God from the error of his way, gives back to his soul[a] life from the dead, and covers over countless sins[b] by their demonstration of love![c]

---

a 5:20 As translated from the Aramaic. The Greek is similar "save his soul from death."
b 5:20 That is, bring about forgiveness of many sins through restoring the person back to God. To cover sins is a Hebrew concept of atonement.
c 5:20 Implied in the context.

About the Translator

D̲r. Brian Simmons is known as a passionate lover of God. After a dramatic conversion to Christ, Brian knew that God was calling him to go to the unreached people of the world and present the gospel of God's grace to all who would listen. With his wife, Candice, and their three children, he spent nearly eight years in the tropical rain forest of the Darien Province of Panama as a church planter, translator, and consultant. Brian was involved in the Paya-Kuna New Testament translation project. He studied linguistics and Bible translation principles with New Tribes Mission. After their ministry in the jungle, Brian was instrumental in planting a thriving church in New England (U.S.), and now travels full time as a speaker and Bible teacher. He has been happily married to Candice for over forty-two years and is known to boast regularly of his children and grandchildren. Brian and Candice may be contacted at:

Facebook.com/passiontranslation
Twitter.com/tPtBible

For more information about the translation project or any of Brian's books, please visit:

thepassiontranslation.com
stairwayministries.org

Notes

Notes

Notes

Notes

Notes

thePassionTranslation.com